HOW TO BREAK INTO
MODELING

VIK ORENSTEIN

Writer's
Digest
Books

Cincinnati, Ohio

To Peter Steinberg
with love and gratitude

Hair by Don Elwood, National Training Director for The Barbers Hairstylists
Makeup by Carroll Britton
Models from the Eleanor Moore and the Susan Wehmann Model and Talent Agencies
Photographed by Erik Rusley

How to Break Into Modeling. Copyright © 1987 by Vik Orenstein. Printed and bound in the United States of America. All rights reserved. No part of this book may be reproduced in any form or by any electronic or mechanical means including information storage and retrieval systems without permission in writing from the publisher, except by a reviewer, who may quote brief passages in a review. Published by Writer's Digest Books, an imprint of F&W Publications, Inc., 1507 Dana Avenue, Cincinnati, Ohio 45207.
92 91 90 89 88 87   5 4 3 2 1

Library of Congress Cataloging-in-Publication Data

Orenstein, Vik, 1960-
  How to break into modeling.

  Includes index.
  1. Models, Fashion—United States. I. Title.
HD6073.M772U56 1987   659.1'52   87-21703
ISBN 0-89879-282-7

Design by Robert Fillie.

ACKNOWLEDGMENTS

I wish to extend my heart-felt thanks to the following people who helped make this book possible:

The agents, who provided interviews and referred the models and talent who appear in the book:

Andrea Hjelm, owner and president, the Eleanor Moore Model and Talent Agency;

Diane Gale, owner and president, the New Faces Agency;

Lisa Plaisance, broadcast booker, the Eleanor Moore Agency;

Julie Polander, print booker, the Eleanor Moore Agency;

Mary Ziebarth, director of print, the Susan Wehmann Agency;

Julie Anderson, director of print and broadcast, the New Faces Agency; and

Lilly Chorolec, broadcast booker, the Susan Wehmann Agency.

Stevie Kozachok, director of print at the Creative Casting Agency, for representing, encouraging, and educating me when I was just beginning to explore the modeling business.

Sue E. Horstman, freelance runway coordinator, for her interview.

The following people who gave special permission to me for use of photos which were originally shot for use by their businesses: Myrna Orensten, owner and president of M. Orensten and Associates Advertising; and Clarence Birkhauser, owner of Hair for All Seasons.

The models:

Mina Almassi	Robin Klein
Matthew Ballentine	Katy Lasley
Freeman T. Beasley, Jr.	Kay Leung
Eve Black	Titus Leung
John Boehnke	Steve Nelson
Delta Brogden, III	Henry Orensten
Angela Claxton	Vivian Orensten
Larry Covin	Stephanie Rogers
Lisa Covin	Barbara Ross
Kathy Crowell	Vicki Samuelson
Lisa Dejoras	Harry Schuman
Lysa Engseth	Muriel Schuman
Susan Fallek	Gini Senser
Tara Flanagan	Charlie Skemp
Joel Garner	Jamie Spence
James Gaulke	Thomas Spence
Monique Gauthier	Leslie Stager
Nancy Hauskins	Regina Williams
Bill Heil	Staci Williams
Christine Heinen	Tom Williams
Traver Hutchins	Barry Yellin
Janice Johnson	Arlene Youngren
Andrew Jurgens	

The artists:
Tara Flanagan, photographic stylist; Leslie Orensten, photographic stylist; and Teresa Dunn, hair and make-up artist.

The parents of the children who modeled for this book: Don and Deb Claxton, and Gayle Steward.

Oscar Collier, who is a top-notch literary agent and a pleasure to work with.

Carol Cartaino, editor-in-chief at Writer's Digest books, who suggested this topic to me.

Connie Eidenier, my editor, who was there through it all.

CONTENTS

WHO CAN BE A MODEL? YOU!

How much do you know about modeling? Take this little quiz to find out.

TRUE/FALSE

1. If you're a woman who wants to become a model, you must be at least 5′10″ and outrageously skinny with legs up to there. If you're a man who aspires to modeling, you have to be a bodybuilder with big muscles, and the taller you are, the better.

2. You must move to Manhattan to become a model.

3. To be a model you must look gorgeous all the time, a 100 percent natural knockout.

4. Fashion work accounts for at least 95 percent of the overall modeling market.

5. Models are usually cute but stupid.

6. If you want to give modeling a try, you have to quit your regular job and risk financial insecurity.

7. It costs thousands of dollars to get started in modeling.

8. Your modeling life span is over when you see your first wrinkle.

9. Models are constantly worried about and fussing over their appearance, even when they're not working.

10. It's always the prettiest gals and the most handsome guys who get the jobs.

If you answered "true" to any of these questions, then you, like many, have believed the myths circulating about this rewarding and little-understood profession. Take a look at the real answers.

1. False. New York City fashion models are usually quite tall, but the average height for models in other cities is much shorter. This is because fashion models in smaller markets must fit into off-the-rack clothing (sizes 6-8 for women, 42R for men). If the model is too tall, the garments won't hang right or they will be too short. For this same reason, men should have excellent muscle tone, but *not bulk*.

For nonfashion work (e.g., character and specialty modeling) models often supply their own wardrobe, and there is no height restriction at all. The skinny look for women in modeling went out in the sixties. Today's buyers prefer a healthier build, and models must reflect this trend.

2. False. There are modeling and talent agencies and modeling jobs where you live or nearby. Those who live in rural areas may have to commute to the nearest urban area to find modeling work, but for most of us, opportunity is only a few minutes away.

Sure, there may be more modeling jobs in New York City or L.A., but there's more competition, too. In smaller cities the pace is less grueling, some standards are less rigid, and your career can last much longer—you won't be over the hill at twenty-five.

3. False. Models are real people, too. Do you think Christie Brinkley wakes up in the morning with her face made up, her hair coiffed, and wearing matching accessories? The models you see in magazines have the best designers in the country, who spend hours planning their photos, making them up, and choosing their wardrobes. More often than not, the final photos are retouched by air-brush. That glamour look is really a combination of three elements: natural beauty, makeup and lighting effects, and personality. Anyone can learn to bring these elements together to become the knockout she or he has always wanted to be.

4. False. Fashion is only a small fraction of the market in most cities. But if you can portray characters (e.g., business types, a young mom or dad, a grandparent) or if you have great hands or legs, there will be plenty of modeling opportunities for you.

5. False. Models who are stupid generally don't get very far. To succeed in modeling you need to be an astute businessperson; you must be creative; you should be sensitive to the moods of photographers and directors; you must be personable, professional, and able to keep orderly records; and you must get to bookings well prepared and on time. I'm not saying that all models are geniuses, but there aren't more dumb bunnies in modeling than there are in any other profession.

6. False. For most people in most cities, modeling is a part-time job. The work pays very well when you can get it, but there generally isn't enough volume to keep all the talent working full-time. In fact, only about 2 percent can depend on modeling for their entire livelihood. So agents expect you to have a "real" job and try to help you work around it. People you see every day are models: students, sales clerks, security guards, even lawyers.

7. False. Of course you can get carried away and spend a fortune shooting an elaborate portfolio and buying cosmetics, accessories, garment bags, and answering machines, but if you are informed about what you need at each stage in your career, you can begin by spending very little, often under a hundred dollars. Then, as you get modeling work, you can gradually add to your portfolio and purchase other items as the needs arise.

8. False. It's true that some Manhattan-based high-fashion models are middle-aged at twenty-five, but in most markets mature models are in great demand. In fact, even more so than their younger counterparts. Your marketability isn't over at twenty-five or thirty-five or even sixty-five; whether you're male or female, it's probably just beginning.

9. False. Although some models dress and make themselves up for everyday wear as though they're going to a shoot, most are actually quite casual about their appearance when they aren't working. Many wear little or no

Muriel, a teacher, has done live, print, and broadcast modeling. Her characters range from businesswoman to crazy washer-woman types.

Charlie first listed with a midwestern modeling agency as broadcast talent when he was a student pursuing a college degree.

Gini's pretty "young mom" look reflects her real life: while she pursues print and broadcast modeling work, her children and husband keep her busy at home!

Traver, a fashion model, also moonlights as a limousine driver for some very famous clients.

makeup and favor comfortable, loose-fitting clothing.

10. False. Being pretty or handsome helps when you're trying to work in fashion modeling, but if a model is late for a booking, unprepared, a prima donna, or otherwise irresponsible, she or he could be the most attractive creature on earth and still not get called back to work again. It's the model who is on time, prepared, friendly, and responsible who gets the jobs.

Now that some of your negative impressions of the field have been dispelled, tell the truth: doesn't modeling sound more tempting as a second career? Haven't you wondered what it would be like to be the center of attention at a pho-

to shoot or to be one of those people in the magazines, ads, and catalogs? Well, it could be you. It's not nearly as unfeasible as you thought it was.

Certainly, keeping the idea a fantasy would be safer; there's no risk of rejection. But wouldn't it feel great to see yourself in your first professional photos? How about the first time a friend calls you to say she saw you in a newspaper ad? And who ever turned up his nose at extra money?

Another benefit of being a model is that you are in business for yourself. The credit, the satisfaction, and the rewards all belong to you—not to a boss, not to a company for which you work.

Eve, whose modeling credits run the gamut from industrial to catalog work, also is a successful insurance sales person.

Yes, there is some financial investment involved, but compared to the overhead of going into almost any other business for yourself, it's a pittance.

So isn't it time to put your fears aside and begin your exciting modeling career?

TWO

THE FANTASY *versus* THE REALITY

We all have fantasies. They're fun, healthy, and creative. They help us get through our mundane daily tasks. If you've ever entertained thoughts about a career as a professional model, you've probably had a fantasy that goes something like this:

> You're walking down the street, minding your own business, when suddenly a talent/modeling agent grabs you by the arm and tells you that you're gorgeous! She wants you to list with her agency. She offers you a multimillion dollar contract, which you accept, of course—you're no fool.
>
> You pose for *Vogue* covers and dazzle the masses at live runway shows. Persons of the opposite sex throw themselves at your feet. You become a pampered, sought-after star, but amazingly you maintain your down-to-earth wit and charm through it all.

Sure, the fantasy is fun. But if you want to make an educated decision about whether to pursue a modeling career, you need to balance that fantasy with reality. That's not to say you should become cynical or lose your enthusiasm. You simply should know what's waiting for you on the road to professional modeling.

In this chapter I'll address the most common modeling fantasies people have expressed to me and attempt to dispel the misconceptions.

BEING DISCOVERED

Yes, it's true that some talent agents stay on the lookout for great, new faces and recruit people when they're walking down the street, at restaurants, at sporting events, and at other public places. This is especially true for older,

male corporate or character types who might never approach an agency on their own because they're unaware that there's a market for their look. But even if you are recruited in this way (and the vast majority of working models are not), your modeling career will not be handed to you on a silver platter. You'll still have to invest money and time to get yourself going. You'll have to work at self-promotion just like the models who approached the agency to get listed. You'll still have to prove you can perform in front of the camera, provide a reasonable wardrobe, get to bookings on time, and project a winning personality.

Some agents don't bother to recruit this way, for a variety of reasons. By just watching someone walk down the street, an agent can't always tell if that person would be a good model. A person may have a very attractive face in person, but become stiff and self-conscious in front of the camera and photograph poorly. Or a person who seems plain in person might have a beauty that comes alive on film or on the runway.

And modeling can be a demanding career, one you have to work at to succeed. Some agents are afraid a person who's picked up off the street won't have the interest or desire to make it in such a demanding field.

On the other hand, some agents say their "discoveries" work out better than the people who come to them because the "discoveries" are more easygoing and they don't desire the status of being a model so much that they project nervousness at auditions nor defeat themselves by trying too hard.

Whichever way you get listed with an agency, either by approaching one or by being approached by an agent, you will have your work cut out for you.

In everyday life, Henry is a pretty normal looking guy.

But for print, film and video, he's had to change his character to portray many different types—from the bemused police officer shown here to an eccentric and agitated sports fanatic.

Barbara's personality is naturally energetic and upbeat.

These qualities come across in
her catalog fashion work.

STARDOM

Some people who try to become models have the mistaken impression that they will be the "star," the most important person at the photo shoot, and that each job will be an opportunity for them to shine. People with this attitude don't last long in the business.

It takes a team to make a photo shoot successful: the photographer, the art director, the technicians, the ad executive, and many others. The model is only one of many team players and is no more special or significant than anyone else. Each has a job to do. The true star of the shoot is the client—the company whose clothing or product is presented by the model. The model is not supposed to draw attention to herself; she should make the clothing or product look its best. Once a model understands this, she's more apt to have a long and lucrative career ahead of her.

GLAMOUR

Yes, there are some glamorous aspects to modeling. Vivian, a woman who became a live runway model at the age of forty-seven, told me she never had a moment that wasn't glamorous. She loved the thrill of working in front of a live audience, the beautiful clothes she modeled, the backstage atmosphere, being helped to change outfits by dressers, and working with choreographers.

It certainly feels glamorous when people recognize you on the street and when friends and even acquaintances cut out your picture from an ad or a catalog and stick it on their refrigerators. "People I barely knew would clip my ads and save them," said Joel, a twenty-five-year-old male fashion model. "At first it was embarrassing. But now I just think it's nice that people are so happy for me."

But much of the business of modeling is not glamorous. Even fashion shoots can leave a person feeling more ridiculous than beautiful. For instance, there's the case of a young man who was being photographed from the waist down, wearing slacks, for a Sunday supplement. He was asked to pose sitting with his legs crossed. When he crossed his legs, a natural wrinkle appeared in the fabric. The art director didn't want any wrinkles to be visible, so the unfortunate model had to sit perfectly still while the art director went to work stuffing wads of cotton down his pants and sheets of cardboard up his pant legs to smooth them out. He was amazingly pragmatic about the ordeal. "They were paying me to sit there, so I sat there," he said.

Another male model, John, once spent the day on a roadside getting garbage dumped on him, literally up to his neck, for an anti-litter campaign. The sun and the lights were hot. "It got pretty ripe after a few hours," he said.

One character model was in a shoot that took place on location outside of a house of ill repute. He was dressed as a thug who was going through garbage dumpsters. Part-

way through the shoot, the occupants of the house came out and asked the crew to relocate because the proceedings were upsetting their "clients." "If nothing else, it [modeling] gives you lots of stories to tell at parties," remarked the model.

Most of the time, what you lose in glamour, you make up for in fun. A woman who has done both fashion and character work told me, "Oh, the fashion could get a bit boring sometimes. But now that I'm older and can do some wilder characters, I have a great time!"

INSTANT FAME

John told me he went into print modeling and commercial acting because "I thought it would catapult me into the big leagues. You know, today a department store ad, tomorrow Hollywood! I thought I was going to be the next Dustin Hoffman. I wasn't." Although his name didn't become a household word, John did become one of the few lucky and talented people who make a successful living modeling.

Some models do make it from small markets to New York or Paris or the big screen. But as one Minneapolis-based model-cum-actress told me, "Overnight success takes anywhere from five to twenty years."

SPECIAL TREATMENT

Many new models go to their first few auditions and jobs expecting to be treated either like a great talent or a piece of meat. Usually, neither is the case. The people who conduct auditions are professionals, and they expect you to be professional, too. Hence, the atmosphere is most often business-like and polite.

A few models related feeling as if they were objects being scrutinized, but said that when they reminded themselves they were indeed offering products, then they didn't take it as personally. One young woman told me she is always treated well on auditions because she goes into them with a good attitude. "I think of the interviewer as a friend, not an adversary." But an older character model said he got mixed treatment. "If I'm not what they're looking for, I get a noncommittal 'Thank you very much.' But if I'm the look they want, I could walk in nude with a duck on my head and they'd treat me like a long lost brother."

JOBS FALLING INTO YOUR LAP

"My biggest bugaboo," said Diane, owner of a Minneapolis model/talent agency, "is that people think once they're listed with me, the work is just going to fall into their laps. They think I'll call them and say, 'Here are your jobs for the week.' It doesn't work that way. You don't just get sent out for most jobs, you have to audition. Sometimes you have to go to cattle calls where the odds are two-hundred to one against you. You have to go around and show your face to clients, pound the pavement."

JUST SHOWING UP AND LOOKING PRETTY

Many new models are surprised to find out that makeup artists and wardrobe are not usually provided for them. They don't realize that skills will be expected of them beyond just showing up on time and having a pretty face.

In fact, character and fashion models both must learn how to apply their own makeup for black-and-white and color photography. When a makeup artist is available, he or she is often only there to check your makeup and correct minor mistakes, not to create your whole face for you.

Models are also expected to provide certain wardrobe items. For instance, a fashion model might be asked to bring several pairs of slacks, pumps, or other accessories to a booking. In addition, she should also carry with her several pairs of earrings, nude hose, a strapless bra, and dress shields.

A model who often gets calls to do a corporate look should have several classic business suits with accessories, a wedding band, a briefcase, etc. "I always bring half my closet to a shoot," said a model whose agent loves her for always being well prepared. "If they ask for black shoes, I bring tan and brown, too. Chances are they'll choose the opposite of what they asked me to bring."

MAKING MILLIONS

When we think of models, we think of superstars like Cheryl Tiegs and Christie Brinkley who command several thousand dollars a day for their services. But most models do not become millionaires. Yes, the hourly rate is good: it's common to gross $55 to $125 an hour for print work and $333 per day plus residuals for broadcast.

If you worked forty hours a week at that pay, you might have a crack at becoming a millionaire in a few years. But in small markets even the most successful models don't work forty hours a week. And the amount of work you can get varies from season to season and year to year. In other words, the only thing you can count on in this business is that there's nothing you can count on.

Then how do models survive? For most, modeling is simply a supplementary income and other part-time and even full-time jobs are the person's major source of income.

The few people who make their whole income modeling must learn to be extremely good at budgeting. For most fashion models, the busiest times are spring and fall, and slow times are summer and winter. By planning for quiet times and banking money when they're busy, some of them can make it through the year.

"Watching your spending is *so* important in this business," warned Andrea, an agency owner. "You could make fifty thousand dollars one year, get overexposed, and not work at all the next. So you can't run out and buy a luxury mansion. You have to save that money for next year's groceries."

THE TYPICAL MODEL—FOUR VIEWPOINTS

When I first began photographing models for their portfolios, I thought there was probably a typical person who became a model—someone with a typical background, typical personality, and typical appearance, who broke into the field in a typical way. Nothing could be farther from the truth. The better I got to know my photo subjects, the more diverse and fascinating I found them to be. Every one of them has a unique outlook and personality, wild stories to tell, and individual approaches to getting started in the modeling business. Here are four cases in point:

Barbara "I wanted to be a model for all of the old cliché reasons. I thought it would be fun, glamorous, easy money and lots of it," said Barbara, who first began to pursue her modeling career at age twenty-one.

Barbara had several serious strikes against her even before she started. For one thing, her looks are ethnic, which is not a type that's in much demand in the Midwest, where she lives. Also, at 5'5" she was not an ideal height for fashion, but her age range was too young to enable her to be considered for business or young mom type roles. But she decided to give it a try anyway.

Barbara's boyfriend shot some photos for her, and she approached every major agency in town. Many of the agents who saw her were friendly but noncommittal, and she left their offices not knowing whether she would ever hear from them again or not. "That's the pits," Barbara said. "If they'd just say, 'Yes, we'll help promote you' or, 'No thank you, we're not interested,' it would save aspiring models a lot of second-guessing." One agent was not so noncommittal. "She told me I was all wrong. Eyebrows, hair, complexion—you name it, she tore it apart." In spite of all this, Barbara persisted. Finally, she found an agent who was willing to work with her. She helped Barbara get professional pictures and put together a composite photo, gave her a client list, and taught her to promote herself.

Ten months later, Barbara appeared in her first national advertisement. "It was worth the struggle. My next-door neighbor was so excited for me that he brought me a rose and drove me to the booking in a black limo."

Soon after that, Barbara did two editorial fashion

When Joel was fresh out of the Marines, friends, and even strangers, recognized his charm and good looks, and told him he would make an excellent fashion model.

They were right! Joel does justice to every fashion look, from the rugged, denim look shown here, to the most elegant tailored suit.

*Monique is a friendly,
outgoing person off camera.*

*In front of the camera, for ed-
itorial fashion photos, she
turns on the sophistication,
vulnerability, and sass.*

spreads for a small magazine. "We shot the summer spread in winter and the winter spread in summer. So there I was on the roof of this warehouse in a bathing suit, freezing to death. There was still ice on the ground."

Now Barbara realizes modeling is not the glamorous, lucrative career she thought it would be. But she was right about one thing—"It's fun. I'd still go back and do it all over again."

Joel When Joel was twenty-three years old and fresh out of the Marine Corps, friends and acquaintances kept telling him he would make a great model. He thought a career in modeling sounded interesting, but he didn't know where to start.

Finally Joel enrolled in a modeling school. The course cost him six-hundred dollars and lasted eighteen weeks. "With or without school, I would have still broken into the industry. But it gave me confidence and information that otherwise I would have had to build up through on-the-job experience," he said.

Joel registered with an agency immediately after he graduated. He's in both runway and print fashion and has portrayed business types. He has also appeared in two commercials.

"This business is harder than I thought it would be," he said, "There's more competition. There are tons of good-looking men. There's always someone better looking than you, so you really have to sell yourself. Personality is about 50 percent of it."

Joel says modeling is a job like any other job, but he enjoys it. "I've been on shoots where another guy might complain a little about having to stand still for so long or wait around, but I figure that's what they're paying me to do. I could be doing things that are a lot worse."

Monique Monique is a twenty-one-year-old model who has worked in Minneapolis, New York, and Paris. "I guess I got into modeling because I grew up reading *Seventeen* magazine," Monique said. "I started out when I had just turned eighteen, and I was surprised by how easily everything came to me. I was asked to register with most of the agencies I talked to, and I chose one to work with exclusively. I started getting jobs instantly. Then I wound up in New York City, and from there, Europe." Monique had her share of glamorous, exciting moments in New York and Paris, but she recently decided to take a break from it all and move back to the Midwest. "The lifestyle was not conducive to personal growth," she explained. "I had my view of reality shaken. I was only nineteen years old in this adult world, coming across more money than I had ever dealt with before, dining out every night, and nightclubbing. I got a

little depressed—there's not much support for spiritual development in modeling sometimes. So I came back to Minneapolis, and I'm doing some modeling here. The pace is slower, and the people in the industry treat me great. I'm learning to act, and I'm taking the time to complete college. I'm happy with all the choices I've made."

Henry Henry is a fifty-three-year-old character model who works in print and broadcast. He was a theater major in college and acted in community and semiprofessional theaters as a young man, but he gave up the dream of acting to get a "real job" in order to meet the financial responsibilities of a family. He worked selling used cars, then as an inventor of pet and craft products (gathering seventeen patents), then as a security guard. It wasn't until he was fifty-one years old that he broke into the modeling industry.

"I thought modeling was just for pretty, young people. And I thought you had to sit and wait to be discovered. But when I found out there was a good demand for middle-aged, balding, overweight men, I had a variety of character shots done. I went to an agency that held open auditions and specialized in business and character types. They listed me on the spot, and the rest is history."

Henry has portrayed a whole spectrum of characters: top executives, sloppy business stiffs, taxi drivers, dock workers, convicts, mad professors, insane people, a person dying of cancer, and others.

Henry has adjusted to most of the demands of the industry, but there are still some things he says he may never get used to. "There's so much waiting! You audition, then you wait to see if you got the job. Then you get the job, and you wait around on the set until they need you."

And Henry has had his embarrassing moments. During his first "bite and smile" audition, he was videotaped biting into a hamburger bun, smiling into the camera, and saying one line. He left the audition feeling as though he'd done a great job. Then when he got to his car, he looked in his rearview mirror and realized "I had snot on the end of my nose." Henry added, "I didn't get the job."

Then there was the time he had to roll in the dirt because he was playing a dock worker and his denims looked too new. "That was good fun."

But he says the rewards far outweigh the little discomforts. "The people I meet in this business are the cream of the crop; the money's great, when you work; and it's always something new and always a challenge."

THREE

HIDDEN MARKETS

When most people think of modeling, they probably think of fashion because it's the most visible and most glamorized part of the industry. But the majority of modeling work outside of New York and the other fashion capitals is nonfashion work. In some markets, in fact, fashion comprises as little as 2 percent. What, then, is the other 98 percent? These hidden markets are often overlooked by beginning models.

HIDDEN MARKETS

Print Ads Pick up your local newspaper and flip through the pages. Notice the ads for banks, health maintenance organizations (HMOs), hospitals, condominiums, restaurants, and other products and services that feature people in all kinds of real-life pursuits? They appear as doctors, nurses, dentists, bankers and other businesspeople, taxi drivers, senior citizens, young moms and dads, college kids and small children, homeowners and do-it-yourselfers. Those "real people" are almost all professional models. They're all represented by talent agencies just like fashion models are, and they all go on auditions and go-sees to land the roles you see them in.

Television Commercials The same thing is true of the people you see in TV advertisements. The housewife happily scrubbing her toilet bowl, the pet owner stroking his cat, the butcher, the plumber, the postman with the runny nose, the beer drinker—they're all broadcast models.

Catalog In addition to modeling for catalogs that feature clothing and fashions, there is a market for models in cata-logs that sell other merchandise: sporting and camping equipment, gifts, carpentry tools, photographic equipment, and more. Often models in these types of catalogs are depicted demonstrating how to operate the equipment, or they are included simply to add interest to the photographs since we all like to look at people more than objects. Sometimes only the model's hands are shown holding the product.

Trade Publications There are many jobs for models in ads that are never seen by the general public. These ads appear in trade publications, magazines that are circulated only among people within a certain industry. Computer software, pet supplies, dentistry, and advertising are examples of industries with trade publications.

Slide Shows Many large companies produce slide shows in which models are used to introduce procedures and policies to new employees and to demonstrate new products to sales representatives and prospective buyers. Slide shows are also used by hospitals and schools.

Industrial Training Films Industrial training films are used in much the same way as slide shows, but rather than being presented on a series of slides accompanied by an audiotape, the material is presented on videotape or film.

This friendly businessman might appear in any number of ads, slide shows, or broadcast projects for industrial or commercial clients.

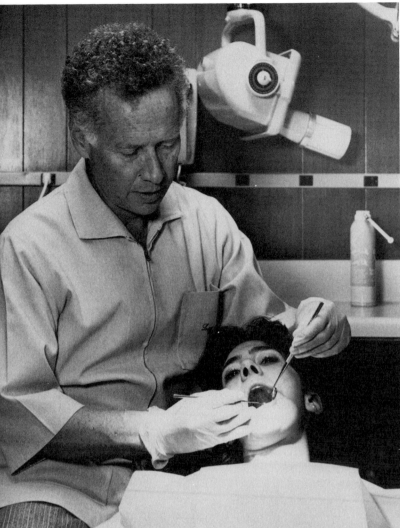

A model may be hired to portray a dentist for ads or editorial material appearing in professional journals.

A model might be hired to portray a florist for print or broadcast use.

This beautiful lady below has appeared as a grandmother in a health care industry ad, and might be seen in ads for many other services and products.

This business type might be seen portraying many roles, from a secretary to a CEO.

Notice that pretty young housewife in the grocery store ad, or the cough medicine commercial? She may look like a "real" person, but she's probably a highly paid, professional model, like this one.

This model has portrayed this sloppy business character for industrial and commercial broadcast and print work.

Trade Fairs Models and commercial actors are hired to demonstrate products, answer questions, and distribute information for exhibitors at trade fairs. Memorizing lines to give a presentation or even putting on a singing and dancing performance are occasionally required. On the opposite end of the spectrum, sometimes all the model is required to do is hand out fliers while sitting on an automaker's latest model car as it revolves. Every trade fair experience is different.

"PRETTY" ISN'T EVERYTHING

What types of faces are used in these hidden markets? "Every kind you can think of," said one agent. "We don't want people who are knockouts like fashion models. In fact, for some jobs, a woman can lose out by being too pretty. Many times the client specifically requests models who look MOR (middle of the road)—just a basic, average, pleasant-looking person, someone who could be believable as the young mom next door, a secretary, a nurse. There are some jobs for people who are slightly better-looking than average, but not glamour pusses. There's also a need for people with slightly odd, almost crazy faces—people who can portray wild characters."

What about other restrictions, such as height and weight? "You certainly don't have to be as tall and thin as a fashion model, but you should be reasonably trim (unless being overweight is part of your character) and you shouldn't be extraordinarily tall or short," said an agent, who forgot to consider all of the requirements one day while recruiting a potential new model for her agency. "I was driving down the street when I looked into the car next to me and saw the most elegant, gray-haired businessman. We pulled up to a stoplight and I leapt out of my car, handed him my card, and begged him to make an appointment to come and see me. He called the next day, and when he walked into my office, he was still gorgeous, but he was only 5'4". I hemmed and hawed and finally told him as nicely as possible that his height might be a drawback to a modeling career. Luckily, he laughed. He said he thought that might be the case, but my offer was so intriguing he just had to check it out."

The hidden markets have fewer appearance-related restrictions than fashion, but they demand more versatility from models and often provide a bigger challenge (and the greater satisfaction that comes with it). One thing is certain—no two jobs are ever the same.

One fellow portrayed a man in "the dead-end zone" for an employee slide presentation. He was made up to look like death warmed over, with a chalk-white face and black circles under his eyes. He got some strange looks from people when he went to the cafeteria for lunch!

A different model appeared in a medical supply ad with only her eyes showing; the rest of her was completely

He may look like a construction worker, but he's really a model portraying this character.

covered by surgical scrubs, a mask, and a cap. "No one would believe it was me!"she said.

Still another man had to climb into a huge, white, foam costume to be a sugar monster for an ad that ran in a dental journal.

Then there was the overweight, middle-aged person who was hired to play a heart attack victim in a training film about a hospital emergency room. The model went on a diet and quit smoking as a direct result of that role.

These are just a few examples of situations models find themselves in when they're hired to work in the hidden markets. As you can see, no job can be considered typical. It's a far cry from fashion modeling, but it's enjoyable work and often more lucrative.

FOUR

MODELING
Part Time, High Pay

As I've already mentioned, for most—even the successful—modeling will only be a part-time job. Smaller markets just don't have the volume of business to keep all the models working all the time. This means you'll have to keep your other job as you pursue your modeling career or get a second part-time job to supplement your modeling income.

But what modeling lacks in regular hours, it makes up for in high hourly pay. You're probably wondering, "Exactly how high?" In fact, if you're anything like I was when I first began to explore modeling, you're quivering in anticipation of finding out exactly how much money you can earn as a model. What's the bottom line on the big bucks?

YEARLY INCOME

Many aspiring models ask me, "How much do you think I can earn in my first year? What's the average model's income?" I can only reply, "I haven't the vaguest idea." Even agents will not venture to guess how much any individual can earn, because there are too many variables: the state of the economy, the modeling market in your hometown, your look, your disposition, how hard you work to promote yourself, how hard your agent works to promote you, your level of versatility, whether you get overexposed, whether you have any extra-marketable qualities (for instance, in Minneapolis, agents are particularly interested in models and broadcast actors who have lived and worked in other markets, especially New York City). Luck, of course, is also a factor in any model's success.

So you see, no one can divine what you can earn in a year. However, I can tell you approximately how much you can earn per hour or per day for each of the various types of modeling work.

Print Modeling This branch of modeling incorporates the use of advertisements and commercial ad trade publications, with models portraying fashion, industrial, or character roles.

Advertisements, Commercial or Trade Publications, and Fashion and Nonfashion There is no union for print models, so the rate of pay varies from market to market and model to model. But if you're represented by an agent, you can expect to gross between fifty-five dollars and a hundred and twenty-five dollars per hour. If the job lasts four to eight hours, you will receive a *"day rate,"* which is generally the equivalent of five times your regular hourly rate. If you're not represented by an agent and are freelancing (either by choice or necessity), you will probably make considerably less.

Lingerie, Swimsuits, and Nude Work Payment for this type of work can range from two to three times your regular hourly rate, or it can be negotiated by your agent. Most agents recognize that work involving nudity (for medical journals and other such areas) is very sensitive. For this reason, they often use mature actors and actresses rather than young print models.

Billboard and Other High-Exposure Work Payment can be negotiated by your agent, or it can be billed out at day rate plus hourly. For instance, say you have a regular hourly rate of fifty dollars and your day rate is two hundred and fifty dollars. If you worked at a high exposure job for two hours, you would receive your day rate of two hundred fifty dollars plus a hundred dollars for the two hours you worked. And the total would be three hundred fifty dollars.

Unions Unlike print models, broadcast and film talent have unions to protect them and set standards for their rate of pay nationwide. Screen Actor's Guild (SAG) and American Federation of Television and Radio Artists (AFTRA) are both divisions of the associated Actors and Artists of America. Generally, SAG has jurisdiction over television commercials, movies, and industrial films, and AFTRA covers all work that is broadcast on TV and radio, live entertainment shows, and audio and video recordings. As you can see, their areas of jurisdiction overlap. In areas where there is no SAG office, SAG applications are handled through the local AFTRA office. An actor may belong to one or both of these unions. Occasionally an AFTRA member may be hired for a job by a producer who uses only SAG talent, on the condition that he or she join SAG, or vice versa. Dues and fees are comparable for SAG and AFTRA.

A residual is a payment made to the model each time his commercial or film is aired. The amount of the residual is determined by how often and in what markets the piece is aired, and it is figured in thirteen-week periods. It's hard to predict how much a job will be worth in residuals, but even if an ad isn't aired nationally, it could be worth thousands of dollars to the model for each year it continues to run. Therefore you can see that residuals are potentially a much greater source of income than the initial day rate.

In addition to setting the rate of pay, the unions also protect you from production houses and clients with bad credit ratings, help see that you collect all the payment due you, and offer pension plans as well as health and life insurance coverage to those who make a certain amount of money per year at union jobs.

You take your first step toward joining a union when you are cast in your first union job. At that time you sign a waiver, which states that for the next thirty days you can do as much on-camera work as possible without paying the union a penny. At the end of the 30-day period, you pay your initial fee and become a union member; you can no longer accept non-union work.

Some broadcast models never join a union, thinking there is more non-union work available. However, non-union work pays so poorly in comparison that it would take twenty average non-union jobs to make the same amount of money you would make at one union TV commercial if you were a principal player. A non-union principal can receive as little as one hundred dollars or less per day rate and no residuals. For the same job, a union model might receive $333 per day rate, plus $333 for each thirteen week run in each market. If the broadcast ran only one year in the market, the union player would make $1,332 in residuals.

The rates of pay cited below represent union base, or scale wages. In some cities it is conventional to pay above scale; in others, talent are almost never paid above minimum unless they have some name recognition or celebrity status.

Union Broadcast Modeling

Radio and TV Voice-overs If your voice is used for a TV commercial, but your image is not, this is called voice-over work. Payment is $250.60 per day, plus residuals. If your voice is used for a radio spot, this is also called a voice-over, and payment is $125.10 per day, plus residuals.

On-Camera Narration Appearing on-camera as a narrator is extremely challenging, because you must deliver hundreds to thousands of lines without appearing to be reading them off, or spouting disjointed sentences from memory. The pay is commensurate with the extra effort: $520.00 per day, plus residuals.

Union Industrial Modeling

Films A model/actor in an industrial film will find himself playing a role, such as that of an executive, a laborer, or a young dad, much as he would in a TV commercial. He may have as little as one line or many pages' worth of lines to memorize. Payment is $286.00 per day plus residuals for principals, and $100.00 per day for extras.

Trade Fairs Payment for this type of work varies considerably, depending on what is required of the model. It can range from four hundred dollars per day plus expenses for distributing information to seven hundred fifty dollars per day plus expenses for making a presentation.

Non-Union Broadcast and Industrial Work Since non-union work is unregulated, the payment is impossible to predict. I've talked to people who have appeared as extras in non-union commercials for as little as three dollars toward parking, a hot dog, and coffee. Some of them have appeared as principals for a hundred dollars without residuals for a twelve-hour day of shooting.

Live Fashion Modeling Since live runway models freelance and are generally not represented by agencies, the pay can vary. For a large, well-publicized show in a major department store, you could expect to make up to fifty dollars per hour for the show itself and ten dollars per hour for fittings and rehearsals. For smaller, informal shows in shopping malls or department stores, you could receive ten dollars to twenty dollars per show or you may receive gift certificates good for merchandise from the store as payment. Fees are negotiable for live modeling at merchandise markets or shows put on by manufacturers to introduce new lines to their salespeople.

PAYMENT SCHEDULES

Your agent will usually take 15 percent of your billing rate. For instance, if you're billed out to the client at $70.00, the agent receives $10.50 and you keep $59.50. When you're booked for a print job through your agent, the client pays the agent for your work. The agent retains his percentage and passes the rest on to you. You do not receive payment until your agent does. Therefore, if the client makes payment promptly, you could receive your check in as little as thirty days. Unfortunately, more often than not, it takes sixty to ninety days for the model to receive payment.

You can expect to receive payment from union broadcast and industrial work within about two to three workweeks.

It's common to be paid immediately following a live fashion modeling show or within two weeks.

If you're freelancing for any kind of modeling work, be sure to protect yourself by establishing a payment schedule in advance.

Taxes and Deductions The IRS considers models self-employed. This status involves more difficult and complex tax forms. Remember to keep detailed records, including invoices, cancelled checks, and receipts to substantiate your claims to the IRS. It's a good idea to hire a tax consultant or accountant to do your yearly taxes and help you set up a record-keeping system. It could save you money on your taxes and, at the very least, it could help you avoid embarrassment if you're audited.

Deductible Expenses You are allowed to deduct certain professional expenses from your total earnings. Some deductible expenses are:

- Commissions taken from your earnings

- Union fees and dues

- Mileage to and from bookings, appointments with clients and agents, and stores where you made special purchases for bookings

- Portfolio case

- Photographs, composites, business cards, and other promotional materials, including resumes

- Voice tapes

- Costume rentals

Nondeductible Expenses There are certain business and professional expenses you *cannot* deduct on your taxes that might surprise you. For instance, you would think a model could deduct the cost of her makeup, right? Wrong. Any makeup or other personal items that could

be used for nonprofessional purposes are nondeductible. The only exception would be makeup you needed for a specific booking that you would be unable to use in daily life. Pan-Cake, whiteface, and oil paints are a few examples. Here is a list of some surprisingly nondeductible expenses:

- Most makeup

- Haircuts

- Telephone (unless you have a special line that is used only for modeling business calls)

- Answering machine or service (unless used exclusively for modeling business calls)

- Rent (unless you have a room in your home that is used exclusively for modeling business purposes and is separated from the rest of the home by walls

- Wardrobe (unless it's purchased especially for a shoot and cannot be used again, such as a clown suit or period clothes)

A Note About Freebies Should a model accept work that doesn't offer monetary compensation? New, upcoming models frequently ask me, "Should I do a runway show or a print ad for free, in exchange for photos or merchandise?" Of course each situation should be considered individually, but in general, a model can get benefits from doing freebies that are equally, if not more, valuable than money.

Experience Every modeling job you get will give you experience that makes you a more confident, more marketable model.

Exposure Anything you can do to make your face known will promote your career. Freebies help you make contacts with other people in the industry. Each job, paid or not, leads to another, which leads to another, and so on.

Photos Print jobs done in exchange for photos are usually more valuable than getting paid in cash if you consider how much photos would probably cost you. Hiring a photographer usually costs at least seventy dollars per roll of film shot, and more if a location fee is involved. A stylist costs another fifty dollars or so. Throw in the fee for a hairstylist/makeup artist at thirty-five dollars. Say you receive four to six prints that are an average value of ten dollars each. If the photo session lasted two hours and you were paid in cash, you would receive about ninety dollars to a hundred twenty dollars. But you will be receiving photos and services worth, conservatively, a hundred ninety-five dollars. That's not a bad trade-off.

Merchandise Frequently hair salons and small clothing boutiques join forces to give style shows. Just as with freebie print sessions, this arrangement should work out to the model's advantage. Just be sure the hair stylist isn't planning to do anything to your hair that's too new wave or outrageous that would make you lose other modeling work.

THE GREAT BALANCING ACT

Gallivanting all over town taking advantage of the different areas of modeling and, in return, reaping money, experiences, services, and merchandise sounds great, doesn't it? Well it *is* great. There's only one problem. While you're spending time and energy on modeling, your new part-time job, the rest of your responsibilities don't just disappear. You still have your other job or jobs, your family, your hobbies, and your housework. And you still need quiet time for yourself.

So with all these demands on your time, how can you fit in all of it? All the models I spoke with agreed that support from friends and especially family is extremely important. "My wife and kids are proud of me and they're willing to be flexible," said Bill, a nine-year modeling veteran.

Another model, thirty-eight-year-old Freeman, has a wife, two children, a job as a radio announcer, and a busy print and broadcast modeling career. His wife is also a serious career woman, so Freeman has to do his share of the child rearing. His hectic weekday mornings begin when he gets up at 4:00 A.M. He works at the radio station from 6:00 A.M. to 10:00 A.M. Then he's free for auditions and bookings from 10:00 A.M. to 5:00 P.M., when he picks up his children from their day-care center and fixes dinner. In Freeman's words, "It makes for a long day." What is his advice for newcomers to modeling? "Be ready to give 150 percent at home and 150 percent in your careers. Have confidence; be willing to make changes in your lifestyle; and believe in what you're doing."

Other models emphasized the psychological and physical benefits of regular exercise, sensible eating, and plenty of sleep to help keep you sane and healthy even with a lot of demands on your time.

There are certain jobs and lifstyles that fit into a model's schedule better than others. Since most auditions, cattle calls, and bookings occur during regular business hours (weekdays, 8:00 A.M. to 5:00 P.M.), evening and weekend jobs like waiting on tables or ushering at theaters work out very well for models. Phone sales, teaching modeling classes, retail sales, and working for a temporary service are a few more jobs with flexible hours. College students and homemakers are free at various times during weekdays, too. If you're your own boss or own your own business, you can often break away long enough for an audition or modeling job. Some jobs, such as those involving stock work or inventory, only require a certain number of hours per week but you can set your own schedule. Also, if you can find a job in or related to modeling, your boss may be more understanding when you need to go on a shoot. You'll have to use your creativity and do a little hunting to find a job that will allow you the freedom to pursue a modeling career.

How much you can get away with often depends on how well you do your job and how badly you're needed by your employer. If you work extra hard and you've made a place for yourself with your company, your boss will more likely be flexible for you than if you're an average worker or a goof-off.

But sometimes you just can't break away. The agents in small markets understand this. "I know models have to have other jobs to survive in this business, so I can understand if they can't make it to auditions once in a while. But they should never agree to an audition if they're not sure they will be available on the shooting date, just in case they get the job. And if they're unavailable too many times in a row, I'll wonder if they are really serious about modeling. People who are available consistently are the ones I'll call most often for auditions and bookings because they just make my job easier. Anything the model can do to make my job easier will get her more work," said an agent.

It's always important to know your availability before you say yes to anything, even a cattle call. If you agree to an audition thinking you can get out of work but it turns out that you can't and you're a no-show, you risk totally alienating your agent. Many people don't realize that even for cattle calls, your agent gives your name and time slot to the client and the client is expecting to see a certain number of people. If you don't show up, you look bad. And worse, you make your agent look bad.

Although it's difficult to juggle two jobs and other responsibilities, it's important for models to keep a source of income that's more reliable than modeling. Then, if modeling works out well, the income from it will be icing on the cake.

FIVE

IS MODELING SCHOOL FOR YOU?

Modeling school courses cover everything from self-esteem and skin care to voice projection and modeling for television. The complete courses run from eighteen weeks to nine months and cost six hundred dollars to more than a thousand dollars.

The big, burning questions on everybody's mind are: Is modeling school a direct pathway to professional fashion modeling? Will being a modeling school graduate help me get registered with an agency and get professional modeling work?

To these questions, all of the agents I spoke with answered an emphatic "No!" Here are some of their remarks:

> "They promise too much. They lead kids to believe that if they take these courses, they'll be models. I attend the graduations at certain schools to recruit for this agency, but what I find there is that maybe one or two out of a hundred graduates really have any modeling potential."

> "Oh, they teach some practical skills—makeup, runway, posture—but nothing that couldn't be learned from practical experience or from an older, more established model."

> "They'll accept *anyone*, no matter how little modeling potential they have. They get away with it by claiming to be not just a modeling school, but a 'school of self-esteem.' "

Even the teachers from various modeling schools I spoke with admitted that graduating from their program is no free ride to success:

> "Not all my students will be working models when they graduate," says Bill, who teaches courses to male fashion models for a national school. "They will be more confident and better able to interview for jobs of all types; they will know how to take care of their skin; they will be better groomed; and they will have better voice projection. In short, they will simply be more marketable people."

> "Modeling school will not make you magically into a fashion model," says John, a voice teacher at a Minneapolis-based school. "But it *will* help you build self-esteem, and that's the foundation you need to succeed in any business and everyday life."

Of the modeling school graduates I interviewed, none felt cheated. All of them told me they enjoyed the classes a great deal and picked up information that was valuable to them in some way. However, only one of the graduates I spoke with, Joel, was actually working as a fashion model. Joel was earning an amazing average of two hundred dollars per week. $9,600/yr

> "When I graduated, they gave me a list of agencies to visit, and I had some photos from the classes to show them," Joel says. "But I would have gotten listed regardless of the schooling. What it did do for me was to give me self-confidence that came from knowing about the ins and outs of the business. And it broadened my goals within the industry and my approach to striving toward these goals. I would do it all over again."

> "I don't think so," says Katy, a very successful mid-

western model when asked if she thinks attending modeling school would have helped make her even more successful. "I have been approached by modeling schools to teach classes for them. I think it would be lots of fun for a short time, but the schools want a long-term commitment."

"The school helped to get me several freebies—jobs for malls and hair salons," says Kim. "At the free jobs, I met people and made contacts that later led to two or three paying jobs. The school certainly helped me get those jobs. Without it, I doubt I would have even pursued modeling at all. I think it was very worthwhile."

RECRUITING TACTICS

One of the complaints about modeling schools that came up frequently among agents and models alike was that many of the schools use unorthodox methods to recruit students.

One way they do this is the old bait and switch. They advertise as though they are an agency looking for new faces. When aspiring models come in to get registered, the schools sell them a modeling course instead. "I call it the used car end of this business," said one model.

The typical hard sell is another recruiting method that offends many people. If you call a modeling school to ask for information, prepare yourself to answer all their questions before they'll be willing to answer any of yours. Most insist on getting your name, age, phone number, address, and who referred you to them before they'll tell you anything about their school. They may transfer your call on the spot to a professional salesperson who will advise you to come in immediately for an interview and a tour of the facilities. If you request only an informational brochure about the school, expect one or more follow-up calls within the week. For people who don't like to be pressured, this kind of selling technique can be a real turnoff.

My own impressions of modeling schools grew out of my interviews with models, agents, teachers, and students, as well as my experiences shooting pictures for several modeling school classes. The students in these classes, especially the teenaged girls, seemed to be having the time of their lives. They laughed and fussed and helped each other with their wardrobes, hair, and makeup. They seemed to have developed warm, friendly support groups, and they had good relationships with their teachers, as well.

But they seemed overly dependent on their instructors for feedback and encouragement. The teacher of a class I was scheduled to photograph gave instructions to start without her since she would be arriving forty minutes late. Try as I might, the students flatly refused to shoot without their teacher present.

Proportionately, I don't think there were any more potential fashion models in these classes than you would find at a college sporting event or a movie theater.

My main pet peeve about the schools is that they are simply not cost-effective. The average course costs about a thousand dollars. If you get work as a professional model, the earnings from many of your first jobs will go toward recouping that expenditure. That's in addition to other expenses you'll incur along the way, such as expanding your portfolio, printing composites, and getting an answering service or machine.

Who would most benefit from attending modeling school? Someone who's terribly shy, who needs to be drawn out. Someone who already has the physical attributes to become a model, but who needs confidence and polish. "But you don't come out after one nine-month course with a great personality if you don't have the raw material to start with," said Mary, a model.

Taking just one or two courses you think you'd like to try, such as runway modeling or makeup, could be a happy medium between going into an agent interview cold and the other extreme—spending the time and money to complete a nine-month program. Most schools offer individual courses at reduced rates.

ALTERNATIVES TO MODELING SCHOOL

There are alternatives to modeling school that are highly recommended by models and agents alike. Acting and speaking classes can help build confidence by forcing you to stand up and perform in front of people. They also recommend dance classes to improve posture, help posing technique, and tone the body. You don't have to be a great or even a good dancer for a dancing class to help make you a better model.

And often agents can refer you to professional models who will tutor you informally in runway, makeup application, and more, for a small fee.

There are also many things you can do on your own to prepare for a career in modeling. Study every Sunday supplement and catalog you can get your hands on. Analyze the fashion spreads and ads in magazines. Then ask a friend who has a camera, even a snapshooter, to take pictures of you at a shopping mall, park, or another place where there are lots of people around so you'll get used to the feeling of performing. Re-create some of the poses on your own. Try some of your own poses, too. Then study your pictures as you did the catalogs and magazines to determine which of your poses were successful and which weren't.

All of these learning tools are far less costly than modeling school, and they're equally helpful to you in your pursuit of a modeling career.

SIX

MAKEUP

A few of the new models my husband and I photograph are very nervous about doing their own makeup for their portfolio pictures, and some of them opt to hire professional makeup artists. There are pros and cons to this.

True, if you go to a professional, you'll probably get an excellent makeup job and you'll feel glamorous and confident in front of the camera knowing your face looks picture perfect. But eventually you will have to learn to do your makeup for yourself. If you're too unsure of your skills to do it for your portfolio shots, what will you do if you land a real, paying job? It's simply not cost-effective to hire a makeup artist every time you work as a model. Besides, for some jobs you can get called with as little as a half hour notice. That doesn't leave you any time to go running to your cosmetologist to get your face done. And if you have oily skin, it's a hot day, or you perspire more when you're excited, your $35 makeup job could be ruined in the short time it takes you to drive from your makeup artist to your photo session.

When you take your pictures to an agent, she'll probably ask who did your makeup. It's a point in your favor if you did your own; that tells her she can trust you to look great when she sends you out on a job. There are some agents who recommend that their fashion models hire a makeup/hair stylist for their portfolio and composite shooting. Kate, of the Eleanor Moore Agency in Minneapolis, commented, "The field is so competitive and the model pays so much for these photos, that they should be exquisite. So our people always use professional stylists for their comps and books. But that doesn't mean they can't do their own hair and makeup. They are all experts at it. We always send new, inexperienced people for lessons." So,

even if you hire a makeup artist for your portfolio photo session, you will still have to know how to do your own makeup—and do it well!

I realize that the thought of becoming your own makeup expert is scary; there's so much to learn! The way you should apply your makeup depends on whether you're preparing for a live runway show, a black-and-white photography session, a color photography session, a television commercial, a live interview, or an audition. It also makes a difference whether you're portraying a fashion, business, or character type. Styles of makeup application change from year to year, so you need to stay abreast of the trends while still keeping in mind what is classic and what works best with your skin tone and features. It all sounds intimidating, but it doesn't have to be. Applying makeup isn't a talent anyone is born with. It's a skill, a skill that anyone with the desire and determination can develop.

Instead of showing you the whole, terrifying picture at once, I've broken down each area of makeup application into individual steps you can practice at your own pace.

MAKEUP FOR EVERYDAY WEAR

Skin Care Beautiful skin is an asset for both men and women. Are you guilty of common skin care mistakes?

☐ Do you follow a regular skin care regimen, or do you follow one only when there's a problem?

☐ Do you tan too frequently or tan without moisturizing?

☐ Do you use too much heavy foundation, or use foundation too frequently?

Makeup doesn't have to be heavy to lend an exotic,
high fashion look. Subtle is sexy on this natural beauty.

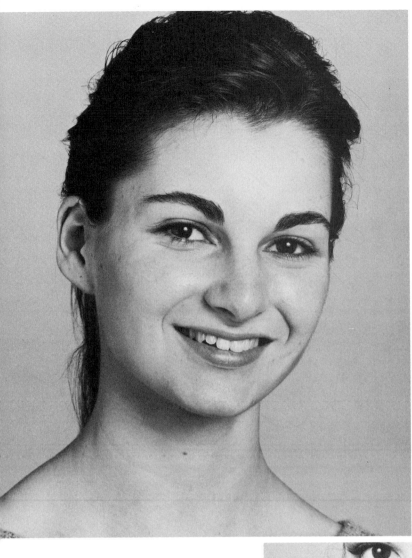

Without makeup, this model's complexion appears drab and uneven. Lips are undefined, and eyes lack emphasis. The face seems broad and flat due to soft, even studio light.

Some makeup that would be overpowering in color, such as the blue eyeshadow and brown lipstick, is just right for black and white. Here, these colors give a nice "MOR" fashion look by defining lips and eyes, evening out skin tone, and enhancing bone structure.

Makeup that seems bright and intense in your mirror, such as bright pink lipstick, will often fade and become flat looking in black-and-white photos.

Colors that mirror the natural pink tone and blue undertones of the skin will look good in color or black and white.

This fashion model uses foundation and powder to even out his skin tone, and a slight amount of eyeliner to emphasize his beautiful eyes.

You should experiment with different skin care products and discover which ones work best for you. Then create your own specialized, daily skin care regimen and *stick to it!* It should become a habit. Are you listening, men? It's not unmasculine to take care of your skin.

Tanning should be avoided, especially by female fashion models. Aside from the obvious fact that it dries and prematurely ages your skin, a fading tan can give you a sallow and even jaundiced appearance. Most photographers prefer fair skin for black-and-white photos; it makes for a higher contrast, a more striking look. Male fashion models are expected to be somewhat darker complected, so a little tanning is OK. Don't overdo it and use moisturizer.

Since your skin is healthiest when it's allowed to breathe, forgo foundation for everyday wear whenever possible. If necessary, just apply a little loose powder with a brush and smooth it in with your fingers for a more finished look.

Eyebrows Eyebrows should be left as natural-looking as possible. The look of full, luxuriant brows is here to stay.

☐ Do you over tweeze?

☐ Do you tweeze so that you overexaggerate the arch and cause a surprised expression?

☐ Do you tweeze the outer third of the brows too heavily, leaving a hook at the inside corners?

☐ Do you pluck the top of the brow?

☐ Do you pluck between the brows, leaving an area that is too wide?

Tweeze straggly hairs between the brows, but *never* pluck brows farther back than the inner corners of the eyes. Remove any stray hairs below the brows. Never tweeze hairs above the brows. Brows should not be

This commercial actress/print model looks natural, but better, with soft makeup she applied herself.

messy. Keep them neat with an eyebrow brush. Apply a small amount of hair spray to the brush, and direct hairs toward the center of the face, against the grain, and then straight up. After a while your brows will become trained and they will lie neatly, naturally.

Some blondes and redheads have pale, indistinct brows. Even some brunettes have brows that are sparse and thin. To darken and emphasize brows, choose an eyebrow pencil or powder that's a shade or two darker than your natural color. Apply with light, feathery, upward strokes. Then blend by brushing the color in with your eyebrow brush.

Eye Shadows Eye shadow should be used sparingly for daytime wear or it will seem garish. It should not be too dark or otherwise overpowering. You want your beautiful eyes to be noticed, not your makeup.

☐ Do you apply solid color from the lid to the brows?

☐ Do you use colors that are too bright or too dark?

☐ Do you wear frosted shadows on crinkly or protruding lids?

☐ Do you wear shadows that match your outfit but clash with skin tone or eye color?

☐ Do you apply shadow too far past the outside corners of the eyes, or not far enough?

☐ Do you apply dark shades too close to the nose?

Don't use one solid color over the entire lid and brow area. Instead, apply a medium-toned shadow in the crease and on the outer third of the lid. Apply a lighter shade, called a *highlighter,* under brows and at the inner corners of the lids. The colors you wear should depend on your skin tone, not on the color of your clothes.

People with pink tones in their skin can wear almost

This male model uses basic makeup—foundation and powder—artfully. Looking at his photo, you don't even know it's there!

any color of shadow. People with yellow or olive tones should wear pinks and plums and avoid brown, coral, and gold shades. Blue-eyed women should not wear bright, blue eye shadow that battles their eye color. Muted grays, greens, and corals can really make their eyes sparkle.

Those who have crinkly and protruding lids should avoid frosted and glittery shadows and stick to a matte finish. Sometimes matte shadows are hard to find, but they're worth the effort.

Bright colors should be used sparingly—perhaps only around the eyes as a powder eye liner or dusted lightly on the brow bone. Color combinations that look great in advertisements don't always translate well to real life.

Under Eye Cover-Up Cover-up or concealer is used to hide dark shadows under the eyes.

☐ Do you apply concealer too heavily and not blend well enough?

☐ Do you use concealer that is of too light a shade?

☐ Do you neglect to apply cover-up at the inner corners next to the nose?

☐ Do you apply concealer too high under lower lashes, causing liner and mascara to bleed?

☐ Do you use an under eye concealer to cover blemishes?

Your under eye concealer should be no more than one shade lighter than your natural skin tone and foundation. Many people use a cover-up that's too light, and it gives them a raccoon-like appearance. Don't apply concealer in a solid line, dot it sparingly under the eyes. And don't forget the inside corners next to your nose. Bringing concealer up too high into lower lashes can cause liner and mascara to bleed. Blend very gently, using short, easy strokes toward the nose. If your concealer tends to creep into creases, set it with a small amount of powder. Concealer should never be used to cover up blemishes; the light color highlights rather than hides them.

Eyeliner Eyeliner should be applied in a soft, smudged line or dotted on at the base of the lashes to accent your eyes. Be careful of making common mistakes with eyeliner.

☐ If you're fair-haired, do you use black liner?

☐ Do you apply liner in a line that is too uniform?

☐ Do you extend liner too far out at the sides of your eyes?

☐ Do you use too much liner?

Never apply liner to the inner rim of the lids; that's passé, and it can make eyes look small. Powders, pencils, and crayons work best. Avoid liquid liner, which can create a look that is too harsh. Don't extend liner too far up or out at the sides; the cat-woman look is long gone. Black is all right for darker haired women but, for most of us, brownish black, brown, gray, and deep blues are dark enough. Plum, heather, forest green, and gold liners can add a contemporary touch.

Mascara Your lashes will look fuller and longer with properly applied mascara.

☐ Do you not allow mascara to dry between coats?

☐ Do you apply too many coats?

☐ Do you concentrate too much mascara at the ends of lashes, creating balls?

☐ Do you neglect outer and lower lashes?

Mascara should look natural, not clumpy or spiky. For a silky look, apply three very light coats, allowing each coat to dry before adding the next. Don't neglect those lower lashes; use the tip of the wand for better control. For more fullness at the base of the lashes, roll mascara on by twirling the wand rather than brushing it on. Black is a good color for everyone, but very fair-haired people should use it sparingly. Remember to throw out tubes of mascara after two or three months. Otherwise bacteria can develop that may cause your lashes to fall out.

Cheeks Blusher in the eighties is for adding color and highlighting, not for sculpting bone structure or taking away emphasis from eyes and lips.

☐ Do you apply blusher too low on the cheeks?

☐ Do you blend blusher insufficiently?

☐ Do you use a color that's too dark?

☐ Do you contour with blusher for everyday wear?

☐ Do you extend blusher too far in toward the center of the face?

☐ Do you put blusher on too large an area of the face?

☐ Do you fail to blend blusher back to the hairline?

Dark, heavy, bronze blusher is definitely out. Try going without a blusher entirely if your coloring is good enough, or use a pale, true color extended from the tops of the cheekbones up and back toward the temples. Blend well, and add a coat of loose powder on top.

▲ DO   *This makeup is more dramatic than for an MOR fashion shot, but is not overdone. It's just right for an editorial fashion look.*

▲ DON'T   *The cheeks are too dark, contour is extended too far in toward the nose, eyeliner is out of control, and the shadow is unblended.*

Don't try to contour for daily wear; it looks too obvious. Save the contour for photo sessions.

Blusher should never be applied in farther than the center of your pupils. And you shouldn't try to give yourself a gaunt look by applying dark blusher to your cheek hollows, or you'll look like you're wearing war paint.

Lips Your lips, like your skin, need special care. Lip-colors should be applied with care.

☐ Do you fail to blend lip liner, leaving an obvious outline?

☐ Do you wear garish colors?

☐ Do you use overly wet-looking glosses?

☐ Do you apply color to only part of the lip?

☐ Do you forget to blot lips after applying color?

☐ Do you allow lips to become dry or cracked?

To avoid chapping and cracking, always use Blistex or another moisturizer. Apply it several times daily, especially during the dry, winter months. Lipstick also helps to moisturize.

To make lips appear fuller, use light, bright colors and frosts. To make teeth look whiter, use deep colors with blue or purple undertones, and avoid oranges and corals.

You don't need to line your lips for everyday wear, but do extend the lip color all the way to the edges of lips; don't shortchange yourself by stopping too soon. And don't neglect to apply color to the inside corners of your mouth.

Overly wet-looking lip glosses are out. Stick to lip crayons, pencils, and sticks.

Where to Buy Makeup for Everyday Wear Ideally, you should buy your makeup at a cosmetics counter, where a salesperson can give you information about the products and help you learn to apply them. However, take a look at the saleswoman's makeup first to see if it looks subtle, natural, and polished before you take her advice on color selection or application. If her makeup looks a little overdone, try to explain to her that you're going for a soft look.

Try not to buy prepackaged drugstore cosmetics you can't test. The colors often look very different in the package than they do on your face, and chances are there won't be anyone around to answer your questions about the products.

And beware of "great deals." Cheap eye shadow can look chalky and fade quickly. Cheap lipsticks have dyes in them that can make your lips look raw after the color wears off.

Many hair salons now have makeup artists and their own lines of reasonably priced cosmetics. Often you can get a complete makeup lesson free when you purchase a certain amount of cosmetics. And many cosmetics manufacturers hold special promotions in department stores where you get a free makeover with a purchase.

When you're investing in cosmetics, be sure to also invest in a good set of large brushes. The applicators that come with eye shadow and blusher are usually far too small for blending the colors effectively.

Where to Learn More In addition to listening to cosmetic counter salespeople and professional makeup artists, you can learn more about applying your makeup for everyday wear by watching other people and looking through magazines. When you see a look you like, try to re-create it using your own cosmetics. Remember, though, that everybody's facial structure and personal style is different, and what works for someone else might not work for you. The only way to find out is to experiment.

MAKEUP FOR B&W PHOTOGRAPHY
Applying makeup for black-and-white photo sessions is different in several ways from applying makeup for everyday wear. When preparing for a b&w shoot, it's important to think of your makeup in terms of tones, not colors. It doesn't matter if your eye shadow is green or plum or blue; what matters is this: is it deep or pale green? Is it baby blue or deep royal blue? With b&w film, all colors photograph in shades of gray, black, or white, so it's important that you learn to predict what tone or intensity your makeup will appear in the pictures. This isn't as easy as it sounds; certain types of colors can be deceptive.

For instance, any color with pink in it, including reddish pink, no matter how intense it appears to the eye, will look several shades lighter in a b&w photo. You could use the brightest, most garish shade of pink lipstick for a shoot, only to find that your lips look stark

white in the finished photos. Other colors that photograph similarly are pastels and very bright shades of turquoise.

Do not confuse bright with deep. Bright colors photograph light in b&w, and deep colors photograph dark.

Colors that tend to photograph true to tone are true reds, blue reds, blue purples, blues, and browns and other earth tones.

Black-and-white photography requires heavier makeup than everyday wear. This is because you don't have the advantage of color to add contrast and to define your features. Also, the intense, soft glamour lights used to even out skin texture can also flatten and wash out your features, so it takes extra makeup to bring them back out again.

In order to get a feel for how different cosmetic colors photograph, enlist the help of that friend with the camera again. Buy a roll of b&w film and have your friend photograph you wearing various shades of lipsticks, blushers, shadows, etc. You'll need to figure out a method for recording which colors are in each shot. You can either keep a list of the colors as they're presented or write the names of the colors on sheets of paper with a thick felt-tipped pen and hold up the name of each color as your photograph is taken wearing it.

Foundation Use a foundation that matches your skin tone and blend well at the jawline. A base that's light and affords medium coverage should be adequate for most people. Stage makeup (Pan-Cake) is unnecessary. If you need to cover birthmarks or small scars, use a product that's designed for that purpose; don't try to make a lightweight product do a heavyweight job. Pay special attention to hard-to-reach areas, such as the tip of the nose and nostril flap.

Men generally do not need a foundation. However, a man who has a very dense, dark beard may need to use a special, heavy foundation to cover it up. If he tries to cover five o'clock shadow with a light foundation, he'll just wind up looking like he has a dirty face. Of course, if the beard stubble is a part of his character or look, he needn't cover it at all.

Loose Powder More important than foundation—or any other single part of your makeup kit, for that matter—is loose powder. Powder reduces shine and lends a satiny look to skin. It also helps blend shadows and blusher, and it helps set lipstick. A shiny face can totally ruin a great photo, so always have plenty of loose powder and a large brush with you on shoots.

Eye Shadow For b&w photography, all you need are two colors of shadow: a medium tone and a highlighter. The

*Many men and women have dark pig-
mentation around the eye area and slightly uneven skin tones, as shown here . . .*

*. . . but under-eye cover-up, foundation,
and powder hide imperfections with a natural finish.*

medium color should be a shade of green, brown, or blue to photograph true to tone. The highlighter should be a shade of pale pink, gold, or beige, and should be matte. (Frosted shadows can appear to be perspiration on film.) Apply the shadow the same as you would for everyday wear, but heavier. If you're doing character work or are trying to project a plain-pretty look, you can eliminate the shadow altogether and use foundation and powder instead. If you're doing fashion modeling, you may want to use a darker toned shadow at the outer corners of your lids for a more dramatic feeling. Don't extend your shadow too far out to the sides of your eyes. No matter what kind of look you're trying to achieve, always blend the highlighter and shadow well. Adding a coat of powder over the shadows helps to smooth them out.

Eyeliner Character models can apply their liner similar to the way they would for everyday wear or slightly heavier. Fashion models may want to make their eyes more dramatic by widening the line from the center of the iris to the outer corners on both the upper and lower lids. No matter how heavily you apply your liner, it should be a soft line, not too defined or hard-edged.

Smudging slightly with a Q-tip or fingertip can help with blending. Always apply liner directly at the base of the lashes; don't leave dead space between the liner and lashes. Your liner shouldn't extend too far out at the corners of your eyes.

Mascara Both character and fashion models should use lots of mascara for photo sessions. Apply it as you would for everyday wear, taking care to avoid clumping. Try dusting lashes with loose powder between coats to make them fatter, and apply mascara to both the tops and bottoms of lashes.

Under Eye Cover-Up Concealer should also be applied as you would for everyday wear. Men who have naturally dark pigment around the eye area should use concealer for photo sessions, as well. Even models without dark pigment should purchase some and learn to use it, in case they have a sleepless night before a shoot.

Contour The art of applying contour could have a whole book devoted to it. Since I don't have that much space, I'll give only the most basic advice about how to apply it. Learning to contour your face correctly is the most difficult—and most transforming—aspect of makeup for photography.

Contour can narrow wide noses and shorten long ones. It can put cheekbones where there were none, define jawlines, and streamline plump faces. However, used incorrectly or with too heavy a hand, it can make you look like a paint-by-the-numbers picture. For this reason, it's important to practice contouring patiently until you get it right. For beginners, it may be wise to go without until you're completely confident.

Your contour can be a powder, liquid base, or stick that is no more than two shades darker than your foundation. Highlighter should be no more than one shade lighter than your foundation.

☐ To narrow the nose, apply a line of contour on either side of the nose from the bridge to the tip.

☐ To shorten the nose, apply contour to the very tip of the nose, not coming up over the nostril flaps.

☐ To narrow the face, apply contour to the sides of the face, from the temple to the jawline.

☐ To define the jawline, apply contour just below the jawbone.

☐ To define the cheekbones, apply medium tone blusher on the apples of the cheeks and extend it back to hairline near the temples. Apply highlighter sparingly to the tops of the cheeks. Then apply contour in a triangle below the cheekbones but above the hollow of the cheek, with the broadest part of the triangle at the hairline.

The most important words to remember when contouring are *blend well!* When you're through, you shouldn't be able to see a line where the contour was applied.

With practice, you *can* learn this technique. You will make mistakes at first, but just remember that no one is ever born knowing how to apply makeup.

Lip Color Always apply foundation and powder to lips before applying lip color. Then line the lips with a lip pencil. If you want your lips to appear fuller, start the color just outside your natural lip line. Then fill in the rest of the lips with the pencil, and apply a lipstick or gloss over that. If you already have full lips with a well-defined, even lip line or you're trying to achieve a soft and natural look, you may want to forgo the lip liner.

Remember that pinks and pinkish-reds tend to fade out in b&w, so your lip color should be a medium to dark shade of true red, blue red, purple, or brownish red. If the photographer is using a red filter on the camera to provide whiter skin tones and higher contrast,

your lip color should be brown or purple or blue, since the filter makes red tones disappear entirely.

Buying Makeup for B&W Photography You can buy the makeup that you use for b&w photo sessions from the same places you buy your everyday makeup, but don't expect the salespeople at cosmetic counters to be any help to you in choosing colors or advising you about how to apply them—that is, of course, unless the salesperson is a model herself, which is not uncommon. The makeup artist at your hair salon may also have some experience with makeup for b&w photography. Whoever you ask to help you in this area needs to understand that you want to purchase the cosmetics for use in b&w photos.

MAKEUP FOR COLOR PHOTOGRAPHY AND TELEVISION
The makeup for color photography and for video or film should look soft and natural. Use the same colors you would for everyday wear, but apply them heavier to compensate for brighter lighting. Don't forget the foundation and lots of powder. Use contour sparingly, if at all. If you line your lips, make sure the edges are not darker than the centers.

For more exotic looks in color, such as high fashion, editorial type photos, go through magazines and practice re-creating the looks that are similar to what you want to achieve in your own photos.

MAKEUP FOR AUDITIONS AND INTERVIEWS
It's not necessary to make yourself up for an interview or audition as if you're going to a shoot. You'll probably look overdone or tacky if you show up wearing camera makeup. The agent or client wants to see what you look like in person; she can see how you photograph by looking at your photos. Normal daytime makeup with foundation and powder is quite sufficient.

If you're going for exotic, high fashion work only and you aren't concerned about landing any other type of work, such as character modeling as a businessperson, you can make your face more dramatic, but don't go wild. Understated is always better than overstated for meetings.

Remember that how you or others must apply makeup for different purposes to please clients and agents may not always be the way you would like it, but it's all part of the job.

If you approach each of these areas individually and take your time to learn the segments at your own pace, your confidence will increase, and you'll be a true artist at applying your makeup in almost no time at all.

SEVEN

HAIR

Wearing makeup you don't feel is "you" is one thing—when you're through with the shoot, you just wash the makeup off—but a haircut is more permanent. So is shaving off beards and sideburns.

To make it in modeling, you must have a hairstyle that's neat, versatile, fairly conservative, and one that won't wilt and need retouching with a curling iron every time you draw a breath. If you're a fashion model, you have to be willing to change your hairstyle as the trends change, although character models can get away with changing theirs less frequently.

In most markets, men must be willing to bare their faces; it's clean-shaven or nothing, although a few do manage to have healthy careers even with mustaches.

If your hairstyle (or facial hair) doesn't meet these criteria but you really want to be a model, you will have to be willing to make some changes. Yes, in some cases it is possible to change the look of your hair without actually changing the cut, but it will involve compromise. You will have to be willing to work with your hair to learn new ways of styling it. If you're determined, you can find a hairstyle that's commercial and yet still "you."

Your haircut says a lot about you. It can say, "I'm a professional" or "I'm wild!" or "I mean business" or "I like to party." The same person can look plain or gorgeous with different hairstyles. You can be sophisticated or youthful, sleek or frumpy.

Of course the hairstyle that's right for you depends on a lot of variables: the demands of your market, your type (character or fashion), your face shape, your height, your hair type, and the styles of the time. But there are general guidelines for models' hair.

WOMEN

As I mentioned, women's styles should be neat, versatile, able to appear MOR and free from the need for frequent fussing. Styles shouldn't be so short that they look severe, nor should they be longer than shoulder length. Very long hair isn't as manageable, versatile, or neat-looking as it should be, and it can look too girlish on a mature woman. The only exception to the long hair rule is fashion models during times in the fashion cycle when long hair is "in." Even then, the hair should be worn long only if the model's face is oval or fuller, her chin and nose are not too long, and her hair type is thick and has enough body to hold up without being damaged or weighted down. Just like short hair, long hair should be trimmed every four to six weeks to eliminate damaged ends and "frizzies."

Hair should never look noticeably gelled, teased, or sprayed, and you shouldn't be able to see through gaps in it. A cut should fall into a flattering frame for your face.

For character models, it's important to find a good, classic style that's right for your face. Current trends shouldn't affect your look much. Fashion models should pay more attention to trends, but not fads. Yes, there is a difference. Mohawks and porcupine spikes, shaving one side of your head and dying the other side pink are fads. Chin-length bobs or wedge cuts are trends. A fashion model will never get any work with a fad cut in most cities. She should take note of the trends, but she shouldn't adopt a hairstyle just because it's "in" if it's not flattering to her face or if it's too difficult to maintain. Neither fashion nor character models should get stuck in the past. "If I see one more long shag with big sausage curls around the face, I'll scream," said an agent.

*This model can wear
her hair wild . . .*

*. . . or sleek and
sophisticated . . .*

*. . . but a few messy
hairs at the crown
can ruin any look.*

*This model can wear
her hair smooth
and shiny for
a young mom look . . .*

*. . . and jazz it up for
a night out on the town.*

◀ DO *Nicely styled,
natural looking hair
is a must for fashion
and industrial modeling.*

▶ DON'T *Too much
gel and teasing makes
you look untidy,
not fashionable.*

Hair doesn't have to be outrageous or artificial to make a visual impact. This feminine, fashionable style needs only a blow dryer.

This broadcast actress looks best in a soft, natural hair style.

Freeman is an exception to the "no facial hair" rule for broadcast talent and print models. Even with his bushy mustache, Freeman manages to keep busy portraying all kinds of characters, from top businessmen and young dads to blue collar workers.

Extra curly hair can look unkempt in photos even when it looks neat in person . . .

. . . but by learning to use a blow dryer and a dab of gel, you can tame it down.

MEN

Men's hairstyles, too, should be neat and conservative. Even men who have hair that's straight and smooth and lies nicely need to learn to use a dab of gel or a squirt of hair spray; stray hairs that are barely noticeable in person are emphasized in photos. Men whose hair is excessively curly should learn to blow-dry it straight and have photos taken both ways to give the client a choice.

Since facial hair is generally unacceptable in most cities, if the thought of shaving off your beard sends chills up your spine or if you're hiding a receding chin under there, you'd better think of alternatives to a modeling career. Some men with mustaches get certain kinds of modeling work, but don't hold your breath hoping you'll be one of them; the odds are against you. Some agents list one or two men with huge, full beards for the rare occasions when they receive a call for an old man, a Santa or a Grizzly Adams type, but a person fitting this description shouldn't expect to work very often.

As restrictive as all this might sound, all of the models I've spoken to have managed to settle on styles that suit both their business and personal lives. One man who plays corporate types in slide shows and industrial films looks more like a rock star in everyday life. "I gel back the sides and punk out the top so it stands up. If one of my friends saw me in a film they probably wouldn't even recognize me."

CHANGE OF STYLE

A thirty-five-year-old college teacher sets her hair on orange juice cans for the young mom look, but for everyday wear she lets it air dry and finger scrunches it into waves for that "just rolled out of bed" look. Another model dries his hair straight back and sprays it in place for an anchorman look; for his personal life, he lets the bangs fall down over his forehead in a more natural look.

What's the likelihood that if you list with an agency, they will ask you to change your hairstyle? "It's the most common request I make," answered Mary, an agent. "More than losing a few pounds or reshaping eyebrows or any of that. Especially fashion models. Lots of otherwise beautiful girls come in here with these long, layered messes on their heads that need to be neatened up. Sometimes I just

ask them to get a trim. Sometimes I ask them to get a completely different cut."

When should you change your hairstyle for someone else? If an agent tells you she thinks she could get you work if you change your cut, is that a guarantee? "If someone promises you work if you'll cut your hair, she's talking through her hat. In this business it's impossible to make promises. All I can tell someone is that I think they'll get work and be more marketable with this or that hairstyle. I can't say for certain they will; it's just my personal opinion. Of course, I'm rarely wrong."

"If an agent asks you to cut your hair, do it," said Vannie, a character model who got her start as an actress in Missouri. "My agent talked me into lopping off a foot from my waist-length hair. I cried for two days after that! But now I'm getting modeling work. And I've really learned to love the new style. I can do so many more things with it."

"I shaved my mustache on the advice of my agent," said a young broadcast model. "I don't know if I'm getting any more work as a result or not, because I only had the mustache for a week after I started in the business. But she knew more about that stuff than I did, so I figured I'd just have to trust her judgment."

If you do decide to change your hairstyle, where should you go to get a really good cut? "Not your mother!" said Mary. "Not your girlfriend. You need a professional cut. I have a list of stylists I refer people to. If they want to use their own stylist, that's fine, but they shouldn't go to one of those discount cutting mills. They're too 'iffy.' Sometimes you get a good cut; sometimes you don't."

And be cautious about getting any chemical process, such as perming or coloring. These treatments can be habit-forming. Your first perm or color application might look great, but after perm on top of perm on top of coloring, your hair can get unbelievably damaged. If you need to add a little body to your hair, try a body wave or a dye that's very close to your own natural color, so that when the hair grows out, the difference won't be so noticeable. That way, you can give your hair a break between processing.

It *is* possible to find that perfect style that straddles the balance between what's you and what's commercially salable. It's up to you to find it.

EIGHT

WARDROBE

When you plan your wardrobe for a portfolio photo session, take your time and carefully consider every aspect from the neckline, texture, and tone to the accessories. Like a poor makeup job or messy hair, an untidy wardrobe can render your photos useless as a promotional tool. An overly trendy wardrobe can make pictures outdated quickly. But a well-executed wardrobe can make the difference between just OK shots and great shots that could last you several years or until you change your look. Wardrobe not only sets the style and character of a photo, but it affects the overall composition as well. The following are general rules you can use to help you plan a knockout wardrobe for your photo session.

WARDROBE FOR B&W HEAD SHOTS

Tone Just as with makeup for b&w shots, the tonal value of the clothing, and not the color, is what you need to consider. Just as with makeup, pinks, turquoise, and other bright colors tend to photograph up to several shades lighter than they appear to be in color. Clothing in the middle to dark tonal range works best for head shots because it provides a good contrast to skin tones. Always avoid white and black; these colors print up either under- or overexposed, lose their detail, and create a large, flat void in the photo. Also avoid pastels; they appear white in photos. Deep or dark blues, greens, browns, true or blue reds, and purples are safe choices.

Pattern Remember, your head shot is intended to show off your face, not your outfit or accessories. That's why bold, intense patterns are an absolute no-no. They draw the eye away from the face. A soft, subtle pattern or no pattern at all is best.

Texture Texture can add interest to a photo without the overbearing or distracting qualities of a pattern. Knits with a loose weave or silk and satin-type fabrics that have a slight sheen are excellent.

Layers Don't try to texturize by piling on several layers of clothing for your head shots. They'll make you look bulky and messy. Simplicity is elegance.

Neckline Your collar should be simple and show a little neck. Don't wear cowl necks or turtlenecks for head shots. Neither should you wear collars that stand up and could cover part of your jawline or chin, or that would look fussy or ruffly. By the same token, a neckline that's too deep can run off the bottom of the photo, looking sloppy and breaking up the composition. Necklines that work well for most people are simple boat necks, crew necks, short V necks, simple collars with placket fronts, and small mock-turtlenecks. Polo and safari shirts are especially good for men.

Unconstructed and Oversized Blazers and Tops Unconstructed and oversized tops can look great in person or in a body shot, but they give a sloppy look to a head shot. A blazer with a little tailoring or a more fitted blouse or sweater are better choices.

Shoulder Pads If you're wearing shoulder pads for a head shot, make sure they're lying correctly and not popping up

How To Break Into Modeling

46

▲ DON'T   *This shirt is too big and sloppy, the solid black loses detail, and the high collar shortens the model's neck.*

▲ DON'T   *Solid white loses detail and the necklace pulls attention down and away from the model's face.*

▲ DO   *Choose a fitted sweater, in a good medium tone, with a neckline that reveals some neck.*

or sliding down your shoulders. The photographer is busy framing the shot, focusing, and directing your posing and expressions, so don't rely on him to tell you if your pads aren't lying right. Also, pose with your shoulders angled away from the camera, or you could wind up looking like a quarterback.

Sleeveless Tops Sleeveless tops don't look as sophisticated or clean-lined as tops that have sleeves.

Accessories Use a light touch when choosing accessories for introductory head shots. Earrings should be medium-sized posts, not distracting little dots and not huge, dangling numbers (unless you've already got one or two good introductory head shots and you're trying for a high fashion or artsy looking shot.)

If you wear a necklace, it should be big enough to read well. Thin gold or silver chains and charms are merely distracting. Pearls or medium-sized costume jewelry are better. But the necklace shouldn't be so large that it distracts attention away from your face, and it shouldn't be long enough to run out of the bottom of the photo, drawing the eye along with it. On the other hand, it shouldn't be too short, or it will shorten the line of your neck. The necklace should also be complementary to the neckline of your top; it shouldn't fall into your blouse or battle with the line of a boat neck or a square collar. When in doubt, do without.

Never use flowers or huge hair ornaments or gaudy pins or brooches for an introductory head shot. Men should also avoid wearing jewelry.

Style For all of your shots, try to choose clothing that is classic and flattering to you, and not clothes that are faddish. A trendy outfit may look really hot to you now, but chances are that in a few months you'll look at the photos and say, "Boy, does that shot look dated." Don't make the mistake of choosing wardrobe just because it's in fashion if it's not right for you.

Business Look Head Shots For a business look head shot, a dark gray or navy blue suit is fine, but don't pair it with a white shirt or blouse—that would be too contrasty. Instead, try a shirt or blouse in a medium/light tone. Neckties, bows, and scarves should be neat, well-ironed and well-tied. They should not be too boldly patterned, too dark, or too light.

Resume Head Shots Resume head shots for broadcast models should be simple and friendly. The clothing shouldn't pigeonhole the person into any type or category. A simple polo shirt, a subtle plaid sport shirt, a safari shirt, a dress shirt with a pullover sweater, or casual crew neck and boat-neck tops are good choices for men and women.

WARDROBE FOR B&W FULL-LENGTH SHOTS

There are two different types of full-length shots and both of them fulfill different objectives. The first type, the body shot, is taken in a bathing suit, a leotard, athletic wear, or in rare cases, in lingerie. For men, a simple pair of jeans without a shirt is best. The body shot should show the model's body type and build to best advantage, from head to toe.

The second type, the full-length fashion shot, should show the model's ability to pose and project a mood and energy that shows off his or her clothing to the best advantage. It's less important to show every inch of the body than to highlight modeling skills in the full-length fashion shot.

Since the objectives of both types of full-length shots are different from the objective of head shots, the rules for choosing wardrobe are different, too.

Body Shots Every model who intends to pursue catalog or high fashion work must have a body shot. Leotards are acceptable, but in one agent's words, "They can be too forgiving. A bathing suit is more honest." And lingerie is very difficult to pose in tastefully. So most models wear bathing suits for their body shots.

How can you make your body shot stand out among hundreds of others? Give it an extra creative touch by adding appropriate props and accessories: sunglasses; hats; sarongs; towels; sandals; hair ornaments; flowers; beach umbrellas; large shells; or for a nautical theme, ropes, life preservers, and oars.

Of course, the bathing suit you choose should be exceptionally flattering to your figure. Dark colors slenderize.

Full-Length Fashion Shots Unlike b&w head shots, it's quite all right to have a bold pattern on your clothes for a b&w full-length fashion shot. The emphasis is different; you're displaying the wardrobe, not your face. By the same token, neckline restrictions are less rigid. And for fashion shots, it's fine to layer, especially different textures, and to use unconstructed and oversized tops, padded shoulders, and sleeveless tops.

Accessories can be very important in finishing your look. You must hold yourself back on head shots, but go wild on full-length shots! Use large earrings, necklaces, belts, bulky and patterned scarves, bracelets, hats—whatever enhances the clothing and overall style of the shot. Men can go wild, too.

After you have a good introductory head shot with minimal accessories, you can try a more stylized shot with jewelry, headwraps, or hair ornaments, like this one.

Tone Tone is an even more important consideration for full-length shots than it is for head shots. When you put together an outfit, be sure the tones contrast; clothing that looks very exciting and colorful to the eye can look flat and boring in b&w prints. If you have a particular outfit you would like to use for your photo session, but you're still not sure how it will look in b&w, take a few b&w snapshots of it so you don't flush a lot of money down the drain by using less than perfect wardrobe for your professional pictures. Although solid black or white outfits are still not the best choices for full-length shots, they aren't as taboo as they are for head shots. If you have a black or white dress you wear well, use it.

Style The style of the clothing you choose for your full-length shots is much less restricted than it would be for your head shots; but it is much more important, since it's the center around which your photo is built. Every-

thing—your poses, the location at which you shoot, your mood, and your accessories—hinges on the style of your wardrobe.

Whenever possible, full-length shots should be done on location. Check with your photographer in advance to find out what, if any, locations are available, and plan your wardrobe accordingly.

Your wardrobe doesn't have to match your location; it can contrast. For example, you could get a powerful image wearing rural-looking denim clothes at the opera or wearing elegant evening wear at an auto junkyard. Naturally, matching the wardrobe and location also works well: a bathing suit on a boat or at a marina; a rugged, denim look in the woods.

If you're forced to shoot your full-length shots in the studio (it's hard to shoot a bathing suit shot on location in winter!), then location isn't a factor and the style you choose for your wardrobe is wide open. Just be sure to

▶ DO *The accessories are simple and well planned.*

avoid the pitfalls, such as faddish clothing, mentioned in the head shot section. Also forget the beauty pageant look (formal gowns, white gloves, etc.) because it's a real turnoff for agents and clients.

Neatness It's imperative that the clothing you use for your shoot is in good repair. Wrinkles can ruin a good photo, so always take articles off the hangers and examine them right before a shoot. Touch them up with an iron if necessary. Everything from your hat down to your shoes should look brand new. Scuffs, lint wads, worn spots, and tiny rips will jump right out from the finished photos.

Line Your clothing should fit you perfectly and hang well. If an item is too big, a little pinning or taping in discreet spots could save the situation. But if something is too small, choose something else. Nothing will make it look as though it fits.

WARDROBE FOR COLOR HEAD SHOTS
When you're planning your wardrobe for a color shoot, it's a lot easier to predict the outcome. The rules are less rigid; even white and black are not completely taboo. But all the restrictions regarding neckline, cut, accessories, and pattern still apply. Choose colors for your head shot that will complement your skin tones.

WARDROBE FOR COLOR FULL-LENGTH SHOTS
For full-length shots, almost any color or tone is all right. Just follow the rules about style for b&w, full-length shots.

To some people, all these rules may seem stifling at first. But as you gain experience, you'll find that these restrictions actually give you freedom—the freedom to use your wardrobe to compose beautiful photographs.

*Bare shoulders and
beautiful earrings
are always a safe bet
for a fashion head shot.*

*Wardrobe for fashion head shots can also
be nostalgic, as long as it retains a hint
of contemporary flavor.*

An aloof, dramatic
shot like this can be
a nice contrast to your
introductory head shot.

This scarf draping the model's shoulders
a good choice for a fashion head shot
ecause it's not trendy, so it won't go out
f style in a few months and force you to
vest in new pictures.

Unlike the body shot, a full length fashion shot is intended to highlight modeling talent, and doesn't need to show every inch of the model's figure.

*When choosing your wardrobe, remember,
rich contrasting colors, tones, textures,
and patterns are good in color and in
black and white.*

Wardrobe

This suit appears to fit this model nicely . . .

. . . thanks to some strategic pinning.

*Models need to have
an eye for detail.
Little things like
a wrinkled wardrobe
can ruin a shot.*

*A renegade dress strap near the
model's raised shoulder can also
ruin an otherwise good shot.
Your photographer can retouch
a problem like this, but chances
are he will charge extra for it,
so always check your wardrobe
before you shoot.*

▲ DO   *A model should always wear her clothes . . .*

▲ DON'T   *. . .and not let the clothes wear her! In this shot the fur coat is hiding the model's beautiful face.*

These three shots are examples of wardrobe which can be used for a body shot: a bathing suit with accessories to add visual interest . . .

. . . bike pants and a shorty top—a nice switch from the usual leotard . . .

. . . a lingerie outfit (note that the model's mood and pose are more modest than in these other shots)

Ideally, a wardrobe and location should contrast (above) . . . or blend (below).

If the wardrobe doesn't achieve one of these two effects in combination with the setting, the picture can be uninteresting and flat.

NINE

A WORD ABOUT DIET

Once you've decided to give modeling a try, you might want to crash diet to be as thin as you possibly can. You may be thinking there's no such thing as too thin. Or you may want to be as thin and lithe as the women you see in *Vogue* and *Glamour*. Maybe, like most of us, you're never quite satisfied with your weight—you've always got just three more pounds to go before you're perfect. Or maybe you've somehow gotten the idea that eating nothing but lettuce and drinking diet soda is the price you must pay to be a successful fashion model, so you literally starve yourself.

Well, don't! Crash dieting, aside from the fact that it's dangerous to your health, can mar your appearance more than a couple of real or imagined extra pounds. Severely limiting your caloric intake can ruin your complexion; drain your energy; make your hair dry and lustreless; cause depression and irritability; and cause your body to burn not only fat, but lean tissue as well, making you appear flabby even if you're underweight.

Even if you hadn't planned to crash diet, you probably have a rash of weight questions running through your mind, including the ones I get asked most often:

HOW CAN I KNOW IF I'M THIN ENOUGH?

The size requirements for fashion models are clearly defined and rigid: women must be able to wear an off-the-rack misses size 6 or 8 (there are a few size 10s who have managed to have healthy careers), and junior sizes 5, 7, 9. For men, the requirement is an even more rigid size 40R. Unfortunately, figuring out if you're thin enough for modeling fashions is not the same as figuring out if you're thin enough in "real life." Not all of us were meant to be size

6s, or size 40Rs. When determining your ideal weight, you have to take into consideration bone structure, height, body type, eating and exercise habits, and general health factors. For some women, a size 6 is a healthy and realistic goal. For others, larger sizes are healthiest, and trying to diet down to fashion model sizes could make them anorexic or bulimic.

You have to stand back and take an honest and forgiving look at yourself. If you're large-boned and tall, you get sufficient exercise, and you eat sensibly, yet you're still a woman size 10 or bigger, or a man size 42R or larger, you're probably at a good weight for you. You shouldn't try to starve yourself down to a smaller size for modeling or any other reason. You're not likely to get a lot of work as a fashion model, but all the other, equally gratifying areas of modeling are still open to you.

If, on the other hand, the only exercise you get is walking to your car and your diet is full of fatty foods, including chips and dip every night before bed, then develop an exercise routine and modify your diet—not just for modeling, but for your good health.

There are some things about your body that you might not be able to change with any amount of dieting or exercise, such as large breasts, full hips, or full thighs. These attributes may keep you from being a fashion model, but it shouldn't get you down. The body type required for fashion models in the eighties happens to be very androgynous, so breasts, hips, and thighs are "out," but the standard and politics of beauty are changing all the time. Perhaps very womanly figures will be the trend again. In the meantime, remember that true beauty is true beauty, no matter what the style of the times may be.

CAN YOU BE TOO THIN?

We've all heard the old cliché, "You can't be too rich or too thin." I don't know about the rich part, but it is possible to be too thin. Andrea, an agent, said, "I sometimes see girls in here that are absolutely emaciated, and some of them even claim to be big eaters. I won't represent them. If they show promise or have a wonderful face, I suggest that they increase their caloric intake and exercise and then come back to see me when they look stronger and more energetic."

The Twiggy look is "out." The slender, healthy, and athletic look is "in." Unfortunately, we don't always see ourselves as we really are. Many very thin women see themselves as fat and are constantly struggling to take off pounds they shouldn't.

How can you avoid this trap? For starters, throw away your bathroom scale. Seriously! Instead of using your weight to judge your level of fitness, use your tape measure. Many of us get a magic—and unrealistic—number stuck in our heads that we want to see come up on the scale. Actually, muscle weighs more than fat, so a woman could appear fatter at a lower weight if she's out of shape and thinner at a heavier weight if she has developed more muscle tone. So measurements are a truer indicator of fitness.

Another technique that can help you see yourself less critically and more realistically is to simply stand in front of the mirror and focus your attention on the parts of your body that you genuinely like. Do you have a small waist; long, slender legs; a tight bottom; or adorable feet? Concentrate on your attributes every day until it becomes a habit. The better you feel about your good qualities, the better you'll feel about your body as a whole.

HOW DO MODELS STAY SLIM?

How do professional fashion models maintain that magical size 8? Do they diet more often or follow more restrictive diets than "regular people" do? Are they just naturally slender, or do they struggle like the rest of us?

Most models I spoke to about their eating habits said they didn't actually diet, but they did make it a point to eat sensibly. "What it boils down to is this: just don't eat when you're not hungry. Before I take a bite of something, I ask myself, 'Am I eating this because I'm bored or depressed or because it's the time I normally eat, or am I really hungry?' " said a size 6 fashion model. She says she eats only when she's hungry and she never feels deprived.

None of the models kept a written record of how many calories they consumed a day or followed a formal weight loss or weight maintenance program. They seemed to restrict their fat intake and struggle with weight no more and no less than non-models. However, they did seem to be more consistent about sticking to their self-imposed dietary limitations. One fashion model said, "Sure, I fall off the wagon once in a while and eat a triple fudge sundae or pig out on fries, but not more than once a week. I may seem more concerned about my weight than the average person, but you would, too, if your income depended on it. A businesswoman or saleswoman isn't in danger of having her boss tell her, 'Don't bother coming back to work until you've lost those extra four pounds!' "

Just like non-models, some models maintain their weight effortlessly, eating anything and everything they want, and others are constantly working at it. But as you can see from the profiles below, they all have one thing in common: they work out regularly, whether it's simply walking three miles a day, going to an aerobics class, swimming, weight training, or running.

LISA

HEIGHT: 5'10"

WEIGHT: 128

SIZE: 8

DIET: I don't have any forbidden foods, but I do try to avoid fatty and fried foods. I find that the less I eat them, the less I crave them. French mousse pie used to be my favorite dessert, but I went without it for a year and when I finally had a slice, I didn't like it anymore—too rich! I do abuse caffeine, which I know is no good for me, and I intend to quit soon.

Believe it or not, snacking helps me control my weight. If I have a little snack between meals, I'm not as hungry at mealtime. But if I don't eat anything in between, I'm so hungry by the time I sit down for a meal that I really stuff myself. I'm not sure exactly how many calories I take in on an average day, but I think it's about normal.

HISTORY: I was really skinny until I was about fourteen, when I got a little plump. When people started to imply that I should watch what I ate, I really resented it, because in my mind I was still skinny. Then I finally came to terms with it and started to exercise and cut out one dessert a day. The pounds came right off.

EXERCISE: Running or walking three miles daily, five days a week.

BARBARA

HEIGHT: 5'5"

WEIGHT: 115

SIZE: 5

DIET: I don't eat any red meat, and I try to avoid fatty foods, but I still eat stuff like chips and dip. I usually don't buy things like ice cream or french fries to have around the house, but I do order them sometimes when I eat out. Basically, I eat whatever I want, but not to the point of bursting.

HISTORY: At one point in my life, I was fifteen pounds heavier than I am now. It was during a period of unemployment when I put on most of the weight, so I think it was due mostly to boredom. Then I came down with a severe case of mononucleosis and ate virtually nothing but boiled carrots and potatoes for about a month. The weight came off and stayed off.

EXERCISE: Daily walking, distance varies.

BILL

HEIGHT: 6'1"

WEIGHT: 165

SIZE: 40L

DIET: I have to work on keeping my weight up rather than down—I've just always been very, very slender. I always have a big breakfast; take a multi-vitamin; eat three good, square meals; and snack in between. I avoid salt, saturated fat, caffeine, chocolate, alcohol, and basically everything mood-altering.

HISTORY: Since I've always been on the skinny side, I used to be too critical of my body. But with age I've learned to look at myself positively.

EXERCISE: One-half to three-fourths hour aerobics, one-half to three-fourths hour swimming, one-half to three-fourths hour Universal weights seven days a week.

DELTA

HEIGHT: 6'2"

WEIGHT: 175

SIZE: 40L to 42L

DIET: I eat a lot of fruits and veggies, and I avoid red meat, but I do eat it sometimes. I don't eat a lot of sweets—they deplete minerals from your system. I believe in everything in moderation.

HISTORY: I've never been overweight. In fact, I was a skinny kid, but physically fit. I used to eat anything I wanted. Now I do watch what I eat, but for general health reasons, not to control my weight.

EXERCISE: I do a split routine. I stretch every day fifteen to twenty minutes and work each of the major muscle groups at least twice a week. I have an aerobic workout three to four times a week. I use free weights for the big muscle groups and Nautilus for isolating smaller areas for detail

work. Since I'm a trainer and develop workouts and Nautilus routines for individuals and couples, I really emphasize correct form—quality, not quantity—in all forms of exercise.

BODY IMAGE

We can tell by the stats on models' composites and simply by looking at them, that fashion models are very slim and fit. No one can argue that as a group, they're in better physical shape than the general public. But are their self-images better, too? Do they see themselves as others see them, or are they as insecure about their appearance as the rest of us?

All of the agents and models I interviewed agreed that fashion models are more insecure than the average woman about their appearance and weight. But models are notorious for their beautiful bodies. The media presents them to us as the ideal. They derive their livelihood from the fact that they have the kinds of bodies that the rest of us envy. How then, could they possibly perceive themselves as not beautiful enough?

"We set unattainable goals for ourselves," admitted one fashion model who at one time weighed only 112 at a height of almost 5'9". "If you think your body is OK, you want it to be great. If it's great, you want it to be fabulous. If you can go without one meal today, you can go without two tomorrow. If you can run three miles today, you can run five tomorrow. It never stops."

DANGEROUS DIETS

That's why so many women—not just models—fall into the dangerous traps of eating disorders and fad dieting. But how can you tell if a diet is unsafe? Here are some warning signals.

Diets that limit your caloric intake to under 1,200 calories a day; diets that promise you'll lose more than one to two pounds per week; diets that eliminate entire food groups (you always need well-balanced meals, especially during a time of limited caloric intake); diets that eliminate all carbohydrates should be suspect.

Any diet that limits your caloric intake to a level below what your body normally burns in a day can alter your metabolism and cause you to need fewer calories if you stay on it too long. Or it's possible for you to begin a yo-yo cycle in which you limit your calories until you've lost weight, then you go back to your old eating habits and gain it back and repeat the cycle.

SAFE DIETING

What's a safe diet, then? We seem to have eliminated most of the popular ones. If you genuinely need to lose a few pounds, here's how you can avoid the hazards I mentioned.

Always exercise when you cut back your caloric intake; this will step up your metabolism so your body will burn fat even faster without burning lean tissue. Give yourself plenty of time to lose the weight. Weight that comes off fast usually comes back on fast, but weight that's lost slowly could stay off for a lifetime. Increase your intake of carbohydrates and protein, but decrease your fat intake. Fat is a highly concentrated source of calories, and too much is a potential health threat. Don't eat anything after dinner. Food that is eaten when you're inactive doesn't get burned off completely, so it's stored in the fat cells.

In other words, there's no substitute for good, sensible eating. Most of us can lose weight without significantly limiting the number of calories we take in, but rather by reducing the percentage of fat in those calories. Participate in at least twenty minutes of aerobic exercise three times a week, and any extra pounds will slowly melt away and stay away. Then you won't just look better, you'll feel better. And there is nothing more beautiful than a healthy body.

SLIMMING DOWN BEFORE A SHOOT

What if you don't need to go on a diet, but you want to have an added "edge" when you go to a shoot? What can you do to look and feel like a lean, mean, modeling machine?

There are several things you can do one or two days before a photo session to make yourself look and feel slimmer.

1. Significantly reduce your salt intake. Salt promotes water retention, which can make you feel bloated.

Sometimes cutting back on salt is easier said than done; even if you don't add salt to your food at the table, many foods have surprisingly high sodium contents. Some of these are soft drinks, salad dressings, most canned and processed foods, vegetable juice, tuna, and frozen dinners.

2. If at all possible, don't eat in a restaurant the day or two before a shoot. It's probably to your best advantage to eat fresh food that you've prepared and seasoned yourself. Restaurant food is high in fat and salt, what you want to avoid.

3. And don't drink any alcoholic beverages. They dehydrate your skin and can cause puffiness around the eyes.

4. The night before a session, eat a well-balanced dinner and then don't eat again until breakfast the next morning. Don't skip any meals; low blood sugar equals low energy equals poor performance in front of the camera. Eat a light meal.

DIET FOR GOOD HEALTH

Not everyone can be a size 8, but that doesn't mean you're overweight. Healthy—not skinny—should be your beauty standard. Severely limiting your caloric intake is a quick fix that can have dire consequences on your health and appearance, and your happiness in the long run. The only safe and effective way to achieve an ideal weight is to combine exercise and sensible eating every day of your life. This includes models and non-models alike. If your body feels good and you feel good about your body, then you're as beautiful as you can be.

TEN

FIND YOUR LOOKS

If you're like most of us, you probably have one look that you identify strongly with, one that you consider *really* "you" or that you'd like to really be you. It could be an elegant high-fashion look; a streetwise look; the sexy, Hollywood siren; the young, fresh girl-next-door; or the urban sophisticate.

Many of my clients who are just starting out don't recognize the necessity of versatility, and they try to have me shoot photos for them that are limited to their one look. They don't seem to have the desire—or the courage—to try a variety of looks.

The fact is that the more you limit the ways in which you're able to change your appearance, the fewer jobs you'll be right for and the less you'll work. Under these conditions, your career could stagnate.

"Versatility is so important! A fashion model who can only do a fresh-faced junior will only get sent out on the occasional auditions for Sunday supplements and catalogs. But if the same girl can learn to add a little makeup and subtly change her demeanor, she can do high-fashion editorial, too. Take away makeup and she'd be a college student or even a young mom. Then she'd have five times as many opportunities open to her," said Diane, an agent. And what's true for fashion models goes double for character models.

"We have a fellow who's so versatile he works more than anyone else in his age range I know of. He's been in print (including catalog fashion) and film and commercials, playing businessmen, farmers, young dads, construction workers, CEOs, a dancer in top hat and tails, and even a nerd doing pratfalls [slapstick]. He's everywhere," said another agent.

"You might not always like the looks you're asked to do, or you may not feel that they reflect the true you," said Lisa, a pragmatic fashion model. "Sometimes I feel downright ugly the way I have to make myself up for a job. I see myself as the natural, athletic type, and sometimes I have to do these very made-up, snooty types. But you know what? I laugh all the way to the bank."

If you want to succeed as a model, you'll have to stretch your identity—as one model put it, "prostitute yourself"—somewhat, but where you draw the line is up to you and your conscience. "I protested the Vietnam war, even though I was too young to be drafted," said Bob, a twenty-eight-year-old character model. "Then boom! The first part I'm up for when I register with an agency is a C.O. for an army training film. Talk about existential crisis!"

"I always hated the 'jiggle' reputation that modeling had. So when I got into the field, I swore I'd never do anything that wasn't classy. Wouldn't you know the first audition my agent sent me out on was for a live performance to kick off a new line of cars: I was supposed to wear a bikini, spiked heels, and a sash like a beauty pageant contestant. The guy who auditioned me asked point-blank if I'd be comfortable doing that sort of work, and I had to answer him honestly—'Not on your life!' I didn't get the job. It was the only time I've ever been glad to get rejected," said a Minneapolis model.

These stories are a little extreme. For the most part, being a versatile model doesn't involve making such weighty political and ethical decisions. It's simply a matter of being able to convincingly portray a number of different types.

What are the most marketable types? What looks should

you cultivate to make yourself the most salable? Which looks are best to have represented in your portfolio?

FASHION

Within the area of fashion modeling there are different looks or categories. While the demand for each type varies from market to market, it's safe to say that outside of New York City, the greatest demand is for an easygoing, natural look, which, for the sake of simplicity, we'll call "catalog."

Catalog This look was variously described to me by agents as "plain pretty," "girl next door," and "just like everyone else, only prettier." For this look, the hair should be fairly natural-looking and not overdone. The poses should be natural, and the clothing should be the type you might see advertised by a department store or Juniors shop.

High Fashion This look is more glamorous and sophisticated than catalog. The hair and makeup tend to be more dramatic. The poses are less natural and more editorial. And the clothing is always the latest fashion, from elegant evening wear to outrageous streetwear. The demand for this look is not as great as for catalog in most cities. And when you do get a job of this type, it usually doesn't pay very well. However, it's probably a good idea to have at least one shot like this in your portfolio, if for no other purpose than to demonstrate your versatility by the contrast with your catalog look. It's especially good to have a shot of this type in your book if you're planning to pursue runway work.

A Word About Sleaze There are some people who get the mistaken impression—possibly from men's magazines—that fashion modeling is all about being sexy, teasing, and "strutting your stuff." I've been approached by people wanting topless shoots, shots with nothing on but a feather boa, shots in peek-a-boo lingerie, and some things that are too sleazy to mention. These people actually intend to use these shots to pursue a legitimate modeling career. The fact is that this type of shot is a real turnoff for legitimate agents and clients. Here are some of their comments:

"Shots are sexier if it's left to the imagination. If a girl wants shots that show everything for herself or for her boyfriend, fine, but don't bring them to me. I don't need to see them."

"Fashion models sell clothes, not sex. If you want to be suggestive, do it with your facial expression, your energy, your body language. But leave your clothes on."

"Everyone likes to look at nudes. I do; you do; we all do. But nude shots or sleazy shots will not get you modeling work. Certain lingerie shots are acceptable, but it takes a very experienced model to make it look classy."

So you can see that you won't benefit from lurid or blatantly sexual shots. Stick to the marketable catalog and high-fashion looks for a successful career.

Some fashion models are able to cross over into non-fashion-type looks, such as young mom or business, by going easy on the makeup. These looks may not seem very glamorous or exciting to you at first, but it's very beneficial to cultivate them.

NONFASHION OR CHARACTER

Nonfashion or character work comprises the bulk of the modeling market in most cities. Please don't confuse the word *character* with *unattractive* or *funny-looking*. Some of the most appealing and attractive faces I've photographed are those of character models. Just because you may not have classical or perfectly average features doesn't mean you aren't beautiful. You may not be fashion model material, but that doesn't mean you're a second-rate model. In fact, as a nonfashion or character model, you stand to make much more money than your fashion counterparts because more jobs are open to you. And depending on your age range and type, you may have fewer competitors as well.

For work in this area of modeling, you should develop looks from as many of the following categories as possible:

Business: secretaries, top executives and CEOs, entry-level greenhorns, salespeople.

Family: young moms, young dads, children, teenagers, college students, grandparents, home owners, do-it-yourselfers

Hospital: doctors, nurses, patients, medical technicians

Dental: dentists, hygienists, patients

Blue Collar: taxi drivers, manual laborers, dock workers, foremen, mechanics, movers, and laborers in other service professions

And do some research in your own market. Find out what major industries are in your city and tailor your portfolio accordingly.

Of course, versatility means more than just doing different types of characters. "Age range is important. I don't care how old you are, I just care how old you can do," said Diane. "Most people should be able to do an eight- to ten-year age span, if they work at it."

It will also help your marketability if you're able to do both MOR types as well as wilder characters.

Being able to portray different types involves more than just putting on a uniform and changing your hairstyle. You have to really *be* a secretary or doctor. How can you make yourself more convincing in these roles?

People Watch We're all natural people-watchers; nothing is more fascinating to us than one another. So just do what comes naturally—observe people. When you go to

Here are four different marketable looks for one person: This introductory head shot shows John, a broadcast actor and print model, as a "regular guy," a type you might see in any number of advertisements for different products and services.

John has an excellent business look—very marketable for industrial films and trade publications.

the dentist, watch how he greets you. Does he have any unusual mannerisms? How does he wash his hands?

Say you're eating at a restaurant and there's a woman at the table next to yours. Does she look like a businesswoman or a nurse or a young mom? Make up a story about her. Watch how she brings her cigarette to her mouth. How does she eat? Does she pick at her food? Does she use her silverware European style? Does she pat her hair and apply lipstick when she's through? Really pay attention to the little nuances when you study people.

Practice Put all your observations into action. Try out the mannerisms and facial expressions you noticed in other people in front of the mirror. You may or may not use these tricks and subtleties during a still shoot, but it doesn't matter. Practicing other people's quirks and habits will get you in the habit of being *in character*. You'll see what it feels like to be someone else.

THE FINISHING TOUCHES

Once you've decided which types from the list of most marketable categories you want to be photographed as for your portfolio and you've practiced being those people with gestures and attitudes, take it all the way. Finish up the looks with hair, makeup, and clothes. Say you're going to "do" a nurse for your photo session. Practice fixing your hair as you would if you were a nurse. Would you keep it out of your eyes in a bun or a ponytail? Don't wait until you get to the studio to decide! As a nurse would you do your makeup soft, not overdone? Beg, borrow, or steal a white uniform. It doesn't matter if the nurses at your hospital wear their street clothes to work in rather than uniforms. Sometimes you have to overstate your intentions in photos, and white uniforms tell people, "This is a nurse!"

The same holds true for other types. For instance, the businesswomen in your office may wear dresses and slacks and sweaters to work. One of them may carry her child's blue and white Smurf umbrella when it rains and bring her work home in a ratty, manila folder. But when you portray a businesswoman for your portfolio, you'll wear a dark-toned suit jacket and skirt, a light blouse, and some sort of tie. If you use props, you'll use an adult's umbrella and a real briefcase. You can play the person as a quirky character, but your clothes have to play it straight.

When you find yourself putting together pictures for a career as a nonfashion or character model, you may find you're enjoying yourself even more than you thought you would in the fantasies you used to have about fashion modeling.

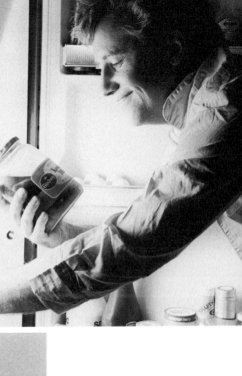

In this product shot, John takes the "regular guy" look one step toward a broader character—as a mussed-up midnight snacker.

He shows his great versatility with a silly character shot.

These shots show four different looks for a 26-year-old woman: This introductory head shot has a relaxed, friendly mood.

This young mom shot could help the model get work in commercial and industrial print media.

This "urban look" fashion shot isn't extremely marketable, but it's an excellent contrast to the young mom photo.

And, of course, the mandatory business shot. Here, the woman appears to be an executive or an architect. She might also benefit from having a shot portraying herself as a secretary or a bank teller, or some similar role.

ELEVEN

Modeling Techniques

Whether you choose a fashion-oriented modeling career or opt to concentrate on character or industrial modeling, it's important to be aware of what poses will work best during a photo shoot. A basic understanding of how the camera "sees" you will help you to avoid some of the common unflattering poses that result in wasted film.

This chapter will give you general guidelines for the two types of shots you will probably encounter first: the introductory head shot and the full-length shot. Once these basics become second nature to you, you will have the confidence to create poses in different settings and situations that will please any photographer.

POSING FOR INTRODUCTORY HEAD SHOTS

When posing for a head shot that will be your main sales tool for approaching agents and later, clients (I call this your introductory head shot), you should pose yourself with your face as straight into the camera as possible. The agents and clients should be able to see what your entire face looks like simply from this single photo. You can turn your face slightly to one side or the other, tip your chin up or lower it somewhat, but any angle that is more drastic than these will not show your whole face, or will show it from a distorted perspective. This might sound limiting to you, but it's really not the position of your face that makes the photo, it's your face itself and your expression and energy. There are 210 muscles in the human face; think of all the amazing subtleties you can project! And you can add movement and interest to the shot, even though you must maintain the head-on position, by angling your head, neck, and shoulders in relation to the camera.

The Neck Concentrate on making your neck look as graceful as possible. Don't let tension ruin your photo session. Common mistakes:

- ☐ Do you keep your posture overly rigid?

- ☐ Do you tense your neck muscles?

- ☐ Do you jut your neck out toward the camera?

- ☐ Do you pull your neck back?

When posing for head shots, your neck should always be in a relaxed, natural position. Your posture should be good, but not "military-ish," or stiff. The muscles in the throat and collar bone area shouldn't be tensed, or they'll look harsh. If you wish to lean toward the camera, do so from the waist rather than leading with your neck, or you'll see foreshortening in the photo, and you'll wind up looking something like a turtle.

The Shoulders In a head shot, the position of your shoulders can add movement and make the photo composition exciting—or make it look like a "Most Wanted" poster.

- ☐ Do you tense or shrug your shoulders?

- ☐ Do you round your shoulders?

- ☐ Do you square your shoulders to the camera?

- ☐ Do you try to move one or both shoulders without allowing the movement to follow throughout the rest of your body?

- ☐ Do you keep your posture too rigid?

▲ DON'T   *The chin is too low and shoulders are flat to the camera, causing the photo to lack movement and interest.*

▲ DO   *The face is square to the camera, and the chin is neither too high nor too low. Her expression is relaxed, yet full of energy. Shoulders are angled away from the camera.*

▲ DON'T *The raised arm is nearer to the camera than the model's face, making it appear too big and directing the armpit toward the camera. Her chin is also too high.*

▲ DO *Arms are raised and directed to either side of the model, not toward the camera.*

The worst thing you can do is just sit there, with your shoulders rounded toward the camera. It doesn't add any interest to the photo, and it can make you appear to be slouching or to be overly big and broad.

Practice isolating your shoulders. Raise your right shoulder, then your left. Right shoulder forward, then left. Then down, then in a circle. Try to shimmy. Notice that each shoulder moves independently on all planes. Keep this in mind when you're making less exaggerated movements while practicing your posing.

The shoulders move independently, but all movement should flow through your entire body. For instance, if you raise your right shoulder, the rest of your body should adjust so your posture is natural and not strained. If you try to raise your right shoulder while keeping the rest of your body rigid, you'll look like the hunchback of Notre Dame.

To practice this flow or continuity of movement, try sitting in a backless chair with good, relaxed posture. Face your head and shoulders straight ahead. Then place your right hand on your hip, and angle your torso slightly from the waist so your right shoulder rises slightly. At the same time you'll feel your left shoulder lower proportionately. Try striking various shoulder positions this way, starting the movement with the arms and torso and allowing the head and neck to fall into position naturally. Use this technique when posing for the camera. Even though the center from which your pose originates (your torso, hands, and arms) will not be visible in the head shot, they'll help you set your shoulders, neck, and head in attractive and comfortable positions.

The Arms Raising one or both arms and putting your hands behind your head is fine as long as you do it in such a way as not to look too "cheesecakey." How you position your arms can make or break a photo session. Common mistakes:

☐ Do you block part of your face with your arm?

☐ Do you create distortion by posing with one arm too near the camera?

▲ DON'T *let your hands obscure any part of your face from the camera.*

◀ DO *use your hands to manipulate wardrobe, props, or your hair in a shot but . . .*

☐ Do you turn your armpit toward the camera?

☐ Do you slouch while leaning on your elbows?

When you're positioned so one shoulder is nearer the camera than the other, raise only the far arm; if you raise the nearer arm, it will seem too big in proportion to the rest of you, and it could block your face from view. Take care not to aim your armpit directly into the camera. If the photographer gives you a table or some other surface to lean on, cross your arms in front of you or lean on your elbows; don't slouch or jut your neck out toward the camera.

The Hands Including the hands in a head shot can help to add interest to the composition and project a mood or feeling. I especially like to incorporate the hands into at least a few shots per roll for beginners, because it seems to make them more comfortable. Although some agents may tell you they prefer head shots without hands, they all find them acceptable if done correctly. Common mistakes:

☐ Do you tense your fingers into a fist or a "claw"?

☐ Do you bend the wrist too much?

☐ Do you press your hand into your face, causing distortion of your face or pushing your chin into an unnatural position?

Try placing a relaxed hand, with the pinky edge toward the camera, up to your face. *Pretend* to rest your chin on it; if you actually rest your face on it, your jaw and cheek will look distorted. Avoid putting the back of your hand or the palm flat toward the camera; this can look too awkward or masculine, and it creates a flat, distracting area in the bottom half of the photo. Your hand, like your neck and shoulders, should be relaxed. The wrist should be held more or less straight with the fingers in a natural position.

The Face In most portfolio head shots, the facial expression and the angle of the face in regard to the camera are governed by the photographer's and the model's creative vision and by the mood of the lighting, the wardrobe, and the background. There are no absolute rules. In the words of one photographer, "Whatever works!"

But the guidelines for the ideal introductory head shot are much more defined.

☐ Do your head shots show you as honestly as possible?

☐ Do you choose poses that accentuate your best facial features?

☐ Do you vary your poses slightly?

In the introductory head shot, the model faces directly into the camera and smiles openly, showing her teeth.

However, the purpose of this shot is not only to show the client as honestly as possible what you look like and how you photograph, but also to show you at your very best. Those of us with very broad faces or noses, or

Some great poses can be achieved when the model is reclining. Here, the model is stretched out on the floor, resting her weight on one elbow.

long chins or noses, might not look our best head-on. Those who have less than perfect teeth or who smile asymmetrically might not look best with a wide smile.

In these cases, it's acceptable to break the head-on, open smile rule. When you do break it, however, do so as subtly as possible. A woman with a wide face who turns slightly to one side for her photo can achieve a pleasing, slenderizing effect. But if she turns too far from the camera, the agent or client will think, "Just what's she trying to hide?"

Here is more general advice for adapting the basic introductory head shot pose to minimize flaws:

Wide face or nose: turn the face slightly away from the camera.

Long nose: keep the chin level with or *very* slightly raised in relation to the camera. Avoid raising it too much, or you'll be looking down your nose at the camera like the Queen Mother.

Overly strong chin [protruding]: keep the chin straight or tilt it down slightly, and face head-on into the camera.

Imperfect teeth or smile: half smile or smile with mouth closed, but be sure you still project energy and friendliness. If your look is high fashion, you might try an expression with parted lips and no smile, but look alert and lively even if the feeling is low-key or sultry.

Once you've established your best angles, work within this framework, but don't stick to it exclusively. For most people it works best to start out a shoot with a head-on pose and then vary your head and shoulder position a tiny bit for each shot, rather than drastically changing your position with each click of the shutter and, as a photographer explained, "flopping all over." Remember that even the smallest movement can give a shot a totally different composition and feeling.

POSING FOR FULL-LENGTH SHOTS

For many of us, posing for a body shot can be more frightening than posing for a head shot because there seems to be so much to think about. What am I saying with my face? How's my posture? What can I do with my hands? Where are my feet? Are my clothes hanging nicely without wrinkles? You can begin to feel like the centipede who couldn't walk anymore after someone asked him which foot he stepped on first.

This is the reason posture is so important; when your posture is good, the rest of the pose will flow into place naturally, without your having to think about it. That's not to say that you can't pose in a calculated slouch or lean if the mood of the shot and the wardrobe call for it. But, there is a correct way to slouch.

▲ DON'T *There is a wrong way to slouch . . .*

▲ DO *. . . and a right way!*

There are two types of posing for body shots, catalog and editorial. Good posture is equally important to both of them.

Catalog For catalog (or natural) posing, the stance is relaxed and the body position reflects real life—you stand, sit, or lie down as you might do naturally at a park, a party, or at the beach. The attitude is casual and not contrived. The mood is friendly, and the model usually smiles into the camera.

Editorial For the second type of posing, editorial, the model must think of herself more as a sculpture than as a body. The poses need not be natural or casual; they should create an interesting form or composition. The mood is frequently more aloof than in catalog posing. The model is less apt to smile or to look directly into the camera. Since in most markets there is much greater demand for catalog work than for editorial, you should have most of your body shots taken in the natural style. Include one or two editorial poses in your portfolio to emphasize versatility.

While these two styles of posing are quite different from each other, there are general rules that apply to both.

Movement Your movements should be side to side, rather than forward (into the camera) and back. If you lean too far forward or bring an arm or a leg toward the camera, it will create distortion. See the photo.

Body Position The theory that the camera adds ten pounds to your figure can sometimes be true, but with correct body position, the opposite can happen. You can make yourself appear your thinnest by angling your hips away from the camera and bringing your torso back so it's flat to the camera. However, if you stand with your hips and legs flat to the camera, and turn your upper torso away, you'll appear bottom heavy. See the photo.

The Feet For most of us, a natural standing position is with the feet approximately shoulder width apart, with the shoulders, hips, and knees squared and weight distributed evenly. This is fine for everyday life, but it makes for a pretty boring picture. Your stance should make a statement. Feet close together and one heel resting against the opposite arch can project gracefulness and femininity. A broad stance can be provocative, powerful, or playful. See the photo.

The Hands Your hands should never hide or distort the clothing you're modeling. Never jam your hands deeply into the pockets, pulling down the garment and causing wrinkles. Put your hands partway into the pockets, with your thumb or a few fingers outside. By the same token, don't pull down on lapels or belt loops. Gesture with them, but use a light touch. And don't cover up clothing by crossing your arms over your chest. This not only breaks up the line of the clothes, but the line of your body as well, making you appear shorter.

The Legs As with the hips and waist, the calves, knees, and thighs look more shapely and slender when angled slightly away from the camera. You can add interest to a photo by shifting your weight onto one leg or the other, by bending one knee slightly, and even by raising one calf in a small "back kick." See the photo.

PRACTICE

Of course it's important to practice all of this before you spend lots of money on professional photos. Try out different poses and facial expressions in front of the mirror. Yes, it might feel silly, but 99 percent of the models I interviewed recommended it for both fashion and character types. Can you think of a better way to find out how different expressions look to the camera and what poses work best for you? Once you know, use a friend with a camera to practice with as suggested in chapter six.

Practice makes perfect. The more you work at posing, the better you'll become. Sheer repetition brings familiarity that makes you relaxed and comfortable, knowing that you're really in control of what you project with your face and body.

▲ DO   *With the hips angled*
slightly away from the camera,
the model looks slender . . .

▲ DON'T   *. . . but with her*
hips flat to the camera, and
slouching, she looks ten
pounds heavier.

An example of catalog posing.
Notice the natural, relaxed at-
titudes and stances.

Two examples of editorial posing. Notice the aloof, pensive
moods in both shots.

Two examples using clothing as props to add interest to photos—especially those shots against a plain seamless backdrop in the studio.

An action shot with leaping, dancing, or other movement can be a nice addition to a junior-type model's portfolio, but it's not a "must."

TWELVE

*T*HE MALE MODEL
Who, When, Where, Why, and How

"A few years ago I had to throw myself on the floor and beg for men to be in my shows," said a coordinator of live runway for a large Minneapolis department store. "But now there are so many trying to break in that I have to turn many of them away."

Most male models work only part-time, as females do. Many work in fitness-related fields as health club trainers, aerobics instructors, and karate teachers. Some do physical labor; construction workers and movers, for example. Yet others work in sales, as lawyers, or in their own businesses. And, like female models, many cultivate other looks in addition to fashion, such as business or young father, in order to get as much modeling work as possible.

WHO
The male fashion model: 5'11"-6'1"; size 40R; age 23-39; athletic and well-toned, but not bulky; proportionately built; rugged and masculine, but not rustic; strong jaw, fine nose, and good lip definition; well-groomed; professional; confident; updated, but not outrageous or faddish, hair style.

This is a composite description of the perfect male fashion model, based on information I gathered from agents, male and female models, and "real people." Of course, there are exceptions to every rule. One man I interviewed, John, who worked as a catalog fashion model, is only 5'9". (He claims to be 6' tall in phone books!) Another fellow, Bill, was nearly 6'3", but still managed to work as a live runway and print model. And there are more men who don't quite fit the ideal in one way or another who still manage to work as fashion models.

"Sure, looks and size have a lot to do with it, but some-

times whether or not you get picked for a job boils down to personality," said Joel, a young man who has both and has modeled in L.A. and the Midwest. "You can make up for an inch here or a flaw there by learning to package yourself and by being pleasant to work with."

The size and appearance requirements for male fashion models may seem restrictive, but in spite of the rather rigid physical requirements, there are more male models than ever before.

WHEN
When is this ideal creature coming into his own? Right now, in the eighties. It's a time when men's fashions are becoming as colorful and volatile as women's fashions, a time when sexuality is being used to sell just about everything in every medium, a time when women have more purchasing power and men are doing more shopping for themselves rather than relying on women to do it for them.

WHERE
Male fashion models are showing up in places where they've never been seen before. In addition to the catalogs and ads where they have traditionally appeared, we're now seeing more and more men in live runway shows. Before, the men in these shows were used mainly as "props" or escorts for the female models, dressed in tuxedos and having no costume changes; now there are shows that feature all men, modeling the latest in men's fashions. One seminational department store has even held runway shows open to the public, in which men modeled a line of bikini and brief underwear. Men appear in ads for cars and

▲ DON'T *This model's head is angled too far toward the camera, with the chin too low.*

▲ DO *The face is square to the camera.*

▲ DON'T   *This model's hand is covering and distorting the face.*

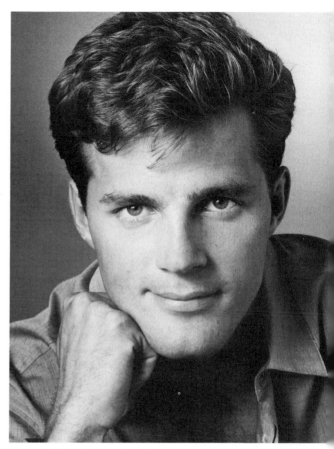

▲ DO   *Here the hand is not interfering with the face.*

linen, both domains once restricted to women. And men's sexuality is used as a selling point in these shows and ads much the same way women's has been in the past; it's common to see an ad with a man in bed, wrapped in a sheet, with the bare expanse of his well-muscled back exposed.

There is even a specialty store in Minneapolis that sells nothing but men's underwear and features huge, back-lit, full-color posters of men in their bikini underwear, shown from every angle. Needless to say, this store attracts a lot of window shoppers!

How do men and women feel about this new phenomenon? "Sex will always be used to sell things, there's no way around it. And if men and women are used in the same way, then that's equality and that's better for all of us. So I don't mind as long as it's beautiful and not pornographic. It has to be in good taste," said Rod, a male model from Omaha, Nebraska.

"What's good for the goose is good for the gander. It used to be that sexual power was the only thing women had. Men had the economic power. So men were attracted to women on the basis of their beauty and women were attracted to men on the basis of their wealth. . . . a bad deal

all around. But now women have economic power, too, and they're saying, 'We like to look at beautiful men,' and the advertisers are responding to this. So I think it's great that men are experiencing this double-edged sword—having power based on their looks on one hand and being scrutinized as sex objects on the other," commented Patty, a young mother.

"I think it's great because it means more work for me," said Joel, a fashion model. "It's all the same—just a job— whether I'm modeling underwear or a business suit. It just pays the bills."

Whether we like it or not, using sex to sell products is a part of our culture, and it's probably here to stay.

WHY

Why are men being used as selling tools in the eighties much as women have been used for decades? Why are men appearing between the sheets, in their skivvies, and on the beach in advertisements?

"People are staying single longer, so both men and women are having to set up housekeeping on their own. When a woman sees an ad with a half-naked man between the sheets, that says to her, 'Buy these sheets and you

▲ DON'T *This smile is too forced and self-conscious.*

▲ DO *Put on a natural and relaxed smile.*

can have the man, too!' When a man sees the same ad, it says to him, 'See, men don't have to have crusty, old sheets! You can have nice things and still be masculine,' " speculated a talent agent.

"Men are finally taking an interest in their own grooming and appearance. And men's fashions are finally catching up with women's. It used to be that if you saw a well-groomed, stylishly dressed, physically toned man walking down the street, you assumed he was gay. Nowadays this isn't the case. And since commercial media reflect real trends, naturally this is going to be evident," said Lisa, a female model.

Others think the trend could be influenced in part by the physical fitness, health, and beauty emphasis of the eighties that's affecting both men and women.

Everybody I interviewed agreed it was simply inevitable. We all like to look at each other; we've always known that women's bodies sell things, and now we've discovered—big surprise—that men's bodies do, too. And we've always known that women like to express themselves with the fashions they wear. Now men have the opportunity to do the same thing.

HOW

So now that you've learned about the new areas of opportunity open to male fashion models, how do you determine whether you have the right stuff? How do you go about grooming yourself to enter this field? And finally, how do you break in once you've decided to give it a try?

Let's go over the physical requirements again that appeared at the beginning of this chapter and list agents' comments on each quality individually. This will help you determine whether you can realistically expect to get work in fashion modeling.

☐ Are you between 5'11"-6'1" tall? Agents may represent male fashion models who were heights that fell slightly outside this range, but they said each inch of deviation weights the odds more heavily against you.

☐ Do you wear a size 40R? This is probably the single most important physical factor. If you can't fit into a size 40R, you will probably have to wave good-bye to your fashion modeling career. "The size and height requirements can cause real problems for us sometimes, because they're almost contrary. If a man is tall enough to

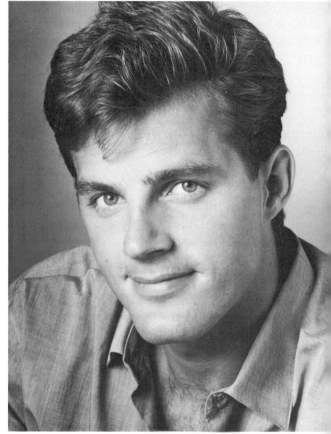

▲ DON'T *Even a serious or pensive shot should have energy. This expression is too low-key.*

▲ DO *This expression is alert, pleasant and open.*

model, he probably needs a size L (long), but he has to fit into a regular. That's why guys who are more slender work well; what they lack in width they can take up in length," said an agent.

☐ Are you between 23 and 39 years of age? It's unlikely that a man under twenty-three will get any fashion work unless he looks unusually mature for his age. However, the upper limits on the age range are constantly being stretched as the youth craze in this country begins to fade. Men and even women can expect their modeling careers to last longer than ever before.

☐ Are you athletic and well-toned, but not bulky? "We get guys in here all the time who look like the incredible hulk and think they're perfect for modeling. Well, that just isn't the look. First off, they simply do not fit the clothes. Second, the average Joe who picks up the catalog is going to see a guy like that modeling the clothes and say, 'No way can I identify with that!' " On the other hand, good tone is a must. A man who's serious about fashion modeling has to have a workout program and stick to it religiously.

☐ Do you have attractive, well-defined facial features? The rugged face with a strong jaw, fine nose, and good lip definition is the general rule, but the overall appeal of a face is sometimes more than the sum of its parts. A man may become a successful fashion model even if he has a feature or two that deviate from the ideal if he has other, perhaps intangible, qualities that compensate. That's something he and his agent must decide. But a male fashion model needs to have even better raw material than his female counterpart, because he can't change or mold his appearance with makeup and hairstyling as readily as she can.

If reading this list has convinced you that you don't have the raw material to make it as a fashion model, take heart! Since fashion is only a small fraction of the market, you'll still have plenty of work open to you as a character model or just as an average, pleasant-looking guy. Remember that the requirements for fashion modeling are extremely narrow, and that just because your look might not fit into this mold, that doesn't mean you aren't handsome and attractive. If you still think you

Sometimes a model must alter his pose to compensate for unusual conditions. In this shot, we used available light which was coming from above. We asked the model to pose with his head tipped back, which eliminated the shadow on the face, and complemented the moodiness of the location.

could have a future in fashion modeling after reading this list, then you've got some work ahead of you.

The following advice is from established male fashion models and their agents on how to prepare yourself for entering the field:

"Learn to take care of your skin," advised Bill, a male model who teaches modeling to men at John Casa Blancas, a national modeling school. "A lot of my students are resistant to developing a skin care routine because they think it's unmasculine or they just don't realize how important it is or they're just plain lazy." This instructor advises his students to use a moisturizer and a toner every day; to drink six-eight glasses of water daily; and to avoid alcoholic beverages, which can dehydrate the skin.

Another model, John, says he can't emphasize enough the need to learn to iron. "Sometimes you get called on for a job with only an hour's notice and you have to bring your own wardrobe. You just don't have the time to run over to Mom's house and ask her to iron your clothes. And if you show up for the job wrinkled, chances are you won't be asked back again."

Everyone emphasized the importance of a regular workout program. "Nobody but *nobody* runs around with a gorgeous body without exercising. You're not born with a great physique, you build it. If you think you've got great tone but you've never lifted a weight or run a mile, you're just kidding yourself," said an agent.

An aerobic exercise, such as running or roller skating, combined with free weight machines is a good combination. Watch out if your choice is biking, because it can create disproportionately large thighs. When using weights, be sure to stick to lighter weights and more repetitions, rather than a few reps with heavier weights, which can build too much bulk.

Posing Practicing poses is even more important for men than it is for women. My experience as a photographer has taught me that male models who are just starting

▲ DON'T   *This pose lacks focus, movement and energy.*

out tend to be stiff and have little body awareness, whereas women seem to fall into poses more easily. This theory was confirmed for me by agents.

"Posture is all important," said Bill, a model. "Men need to learn to use their muscles to accent the line of the clothes and allow them to flow. It's an idea that's hard to grasp at first, but once you get the hang of it, you'll know it because it feels right."

Men's poses differ somewhat from women's poses. Women strive for a slender, graceful look, angling their bodies away from the camera and placing their weight off-center. Men should strive for a more square, angular look. They can achieve this in head shots by placing the shoulders flatter to the camera, squaring the face, and always maintaining good strong posture, attitude, and stance. When a man's hands appear in a shot, the wrists should always be straight with the fingers in a relaxed fist, or the fingers can be straight and held slightly together, almost like a mitten.

Just as for women, having a friend shoot pictures of you is an especially valuable learning tool to help you get a sense of what your body looks like in different poses.

Grooming "Grooming is very important. Men aspiring to modeling careers should pay extra attention to updating their look and taking care of their hands—things that don't come naturally to many men," said Julie, an agent. "They need to learn to apply base and powder, to use gel, to use a hair dryer, and all those things that women probably already know."

Once you've prepared yourself for a try at modeling by following the above advice, the procedure for breaking in is the same as for women: get one or two really good photos and start knocking on the agents' doors.

This is where the who, where, when, why, and how become you in your hometown now because you want an exciting career in modeling through lots of hard work!

▲ DO   *By shifting his weight, looking into the camera, and cre-ating angles with arms and legs, the model creates visual interest.*

◀ DO   *The model has a firm stance, is well-balanced, and has a masculine attitude.*

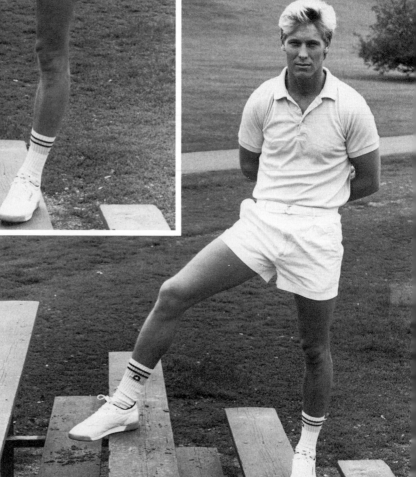

▶ DON'T   *The model is off-balance, and his shoulders are slouched.*

◀ DO *He has good posture, the suit is hanging nicely, there is high energy, and his gesture toward the jacket's cuff is natural.*

▶ DON'T *This model has poor posture, a casual attitude inappropriate to wardrobe, and his lapel is folded up.*

▲ DON'T   *This pose and facial expression are inappropriate to the mood of the wardrobe and location.*

▲ DO   *This casual pose enhances the mood of the photo, featuring the wardrobe to better advantage.*

THIRTEEN

CHILDREN AS MODELS

There is always going to be a demand for child models; of this there is no question. But modeling is a field that even adults can find stressful, full of rejection, and confusing to the self-esteem (feeling on top of the world after getting a job or low and unappealing after losing one.) And modeling is indeed a job—it's real work. Is all this healthy for a young child?

"It can be damaging, there's no doubt about that. That's where the parent plays a crucial role. If the parent looks at each audition as the beginning and the end of the world and takes it very personally when the child doesn't get the job, then no matter how hard the parent tries to put on a happy face, the child will sense her disappointment and feel responsible. But if the parent has a relaxed attitude, doesn't take it to heart when the child doesn't get a job, and tries to make the whole experience a fun one, then the child will be happy," said Lisa, an agent.

"There are cons. It's hard for a little kid to deal with rejection—also acceptance. It can be too much responsibility for them. The child's peers can react supportively or not. And it's hectic for Mom, driving the child to shoots and preparing the wardrobe, etc.

"But there are pros, too. The child can earn money toward her education. She can be given an allowance out of her earnings and learn how to manage money. It's very stimulating and exciting. She learns to be responsible and poised, to interact well and cooperate with people. The time spent preparing for and driving to and from auditions and jobs can be an enjoyable time for parent and child to spend together."

SHOULD YOUR CHILD BE A MODEL?

So there are many benefits as well as potential pitfalls.

Once you are aware of all the potential dangers and have considered all the aspects, if you're still interested, your next question is probably, "How do I know if my child has what it takes to be a model?" After all, everyone's child is the cutest one in the world. Of course parents can't be expected to be objective about their offspring, but the fact is that there is simply no such thing as a homely child; they're all beautiful. So how can you judge whether your child could be the next Ivory baby?

First, before considering your child, stand back and take a good, honest look at yourself. Yes, you.

Do you want your child to model to satisfy your ego?

Would you yourself like to be a model but you're afraid to try?

Do you think having your child model will bring a spark of excitement into your life?

If you can't honestly answer no to all these questions, then you shouldn't try to make your child into a model. But if you can answer no to all of them, then go on to the next questions.

Do you have the time and interest to maintain your child's wardrobe and drive her around to audition after audition after job after audition?

Would you be comfortable taking your child out of school for a half or full day to attend a shoot?

Are you prepared to help your child put into perspective the reactions of friends, relatives, and peers so she won't feel different or special?

If you can answer yes to all these questions, then you can move on to assess your child's potential.

The Ideal Child Model The first thing to consider when trying to decide whether to put your child into modeling is:

*se are two of six babies we
ographed for a health-care
ted project. The babies
supposed to simply sit
play with toys from a
dical" kit. As evident in
photos, some babies en-
performing for the cam-*

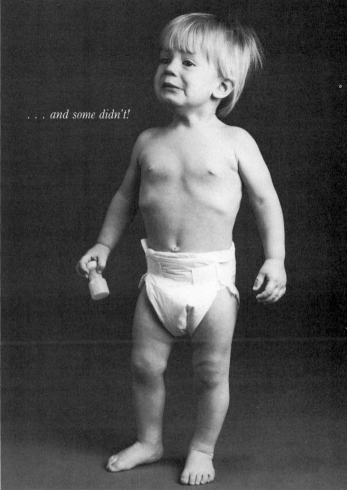

. . . and some didn't!

Does she want to be a model? The best way to find out is to ask her. A child who has no desire to model should not be coerced or wheedled. If she's an unwilling candidate, she'll be under stress, unhappy, and she won't perform up to par.

If the child is genuinely excited about the prospect of working as a model, the next step is to examine her personality and temperament. Is your child outgoing, bright, and a bit of a ham, but not too precocious, "stagey," or affected? Does she warm up to strangers quickly and follow instructions well? Is she gregarious but not too sassy? Does she enjoy a bit of extra attention and appear relaxed and natural in snapshots? If so, she may have the raw material to be a successful, happy, well-adjusted model.

Breaking In If you've determined that you and your child have the interest and temperament to give her a crack at a happy modeling career, the first step is the same as for adult models just breaking in: get photos and approach a modeling agency. Again, the best place to get referrals to photographers is from the agency itself.

The photo, a simple head shot, should be casual and natural. This means *no* makeup. No matter how much I emphasize this during the consultations, there is still the occasional parent who simply refuses to heed my advice and shows up for the shoot with a rouged, lipsticked, totally artificial little girl with hot roller curls. Trust the photographer. And trust your child; her natural beauty is enough.

Once you've submitted the photo to the agency, the interviewing and listing process is also the same as for adults. Remember that when you take your child in for an agent interview, the agent will be assessing you, the parent, as much as she will be assessing your child. A cooperative, calm, pleasant parent is an absolute necessity.

Making Work a Pleasure What can you do to help keep the experience of working as a model happy and relaxed for your little one? First of all, make sure the child eats and sleeps well before a job. If she seems to be getting worn out or frustrated during a shoot, it's all right for you to ask for a five- or ten-minute break on her behalf. Always bring a treat to the set, such as raisins or cookies and juice, so

Children As Models

These two young models, brothers, have a warm rapport with each other that spills over onto the photographer, and the audience viewing the photos.

the child can nibble if she wants to.

Always give the child the power to say no to an audition or job. If she has a field trip or other goings-on at school that she doesn't want to miss or even if she simply doesn't feel like working that day, respect her wishes. However, if the child has already committed to take a job, she should comply. She'll learn responsibility and respect for others this way. If she accepts a job and then turns it down, she won't have a very long career in front of her.

Put away the bulk of the child's earnings for the future, and give her an allowance that is proportionately normal for a child her age. This way her future will be secure and she won't be faced with the dilemma of managing large sums of money before she's old enough to understand how. If she presses you, allow her to purchase a more expensive toy or clothing item occasionally, but try not to let it become a regular occurrence.

If well-meaning friends and family make too big a fuss over the child's modeling, take them aside and explain to them that modeling is just the child's job and she wishes to be treated just the same way as all the other children in the family.

Remember that you, the parent, know your child better than anyone else possibly could. So trust your instincts if you see any signs of stress in your child that may be stemming from modeling. Slow the pace for a while or pull her out of the modeling field entirely if you deem it necessary. Don't rely on the child to tell you when she wants to slow down or quit; she may claim she wants to continue because she thinks it will please you or because she doesn't want to think of herself as a failure or a quitter.

It is possible to give your child a positive, happy experience working as a model if you keep the lines of communication open, stay tuned to your child's needs and desires, and give her the power to say no to a job if she doesn't want to work. You can help her keep the pain of rejection in perspective, as well as the pleasure of acceptance.

FOURTEEN

*T*HE FIRST STEP
Photos

After you've worked on your makeup, hairstyling, and posing skills, what's next? Or should I say, what's first? The first step toward a career in modeling is getting photographs. Even if you're only interested in live modeling, you still need pictures to get started. Most agencies will not meet with you until you have submitted one or two photos to them. If you have pictures, this indicates to the agent that you're serious about modeling and you've done your homework, you're not acting simply on a whim or passing interest. It also lets them see how well you photograph, which in this industry is more important that how you look in person. Approaching an agent without photos is like walking into a medical school, showing them your hands, and saying, "Well, do you think I'd be a good surgeon?"

Some agencies require that you send them a professional, glossy, 8 × 10, b&w head shot; some also request a body shot. Graduation portraits, wedding pictures, and snapshots of you and your friends, you and your parakeet, or you with an exotic and overpowering background are unacceptable.

Some agencies require only a good, in focus, close-up snapshot or Polaroid photo, but I advise against this for several reasons. Your photo is the first impression the agent will have of you. If it's not a good one, it'll be the last. The natural sun and direct flash used in snapshots is harsh and never shows your face at its best. For head shots, professional photographers use soft, even studio light, which portrays you at your best without being deceptive about your true appearance.

Many of my clients are thrilled and amazed when they see fashion photos of themselves for the first time. They often say, "Is that really me? I didn't know I could look that glamorous!" So put your best foot forward—start out with a good, professional head shot. If you're serious about modeling, you'll need professional photos eventually, anyway.

However, if you must begin with nonprofessional photos, here's some advice. Black-and-white film will look more professional than color. Try to have the shots taken with a 35 mm camera, as this will give you superior quality prints. The photographer should frame the shots as tightly as possible, so your whole face or your whole body fill the picture. When the photographer is using available light (sunlight, window light, etc.), he or she should use a large white or matte silver piece of tagboard as a reflector to fill in shadows for a more even skin tone. When using a flash unit, the photographer should bounce the strobe off the ceiling or a wall rather than pointing it directly at the subject for a softer look. For head shots, if the photographer overexposes the shots one f-stop from the meter reading, there will be better contrast in the skin tones.

I recommend shooting the photos indoors, because the light is easier to control. The subject should be positioned two to three feet away from a blank white wall or a blank white sheet of tagboard.

If you elect to shoot the photos outdoors, be sure that the background is simple and does not distract from the subject. If the sunlight is coming from directly overhead, have a helper shade the model by holding a dark toned sheet of tagboard over her head, out of camera range. If the sun is low in the sky, position the subject facing into it; if you choose to backlight the subject, remember to overexpose at least two f-stops to provide natural skin tones.

These two shots demonstrate the first and most important elements in a fashion model's portfolio: a good introductory head shot . . .

. . . and a good body shot.

On an overcast day, the light is even and you can position the subject with more freedom.

"Pictures are so important; I can't emphasize it enough," said Andrea, an agent. "They're our biggest selling tool. If you have beautiful shots, you look good and we look good. It makes the job of promoting you so much easier. I hate to send photos to a client and have to say, 'Please believe me when I say that this girl is so much prettier than her pictures. Why don't you give her a try?' "

You don't need to get an entire portfolio shot to begin with. Agents are well aware of the costs involved, and many are happiest when they see only one or two shots initially. Then, once they determine that you have a future in modeling, they'll guide you in planning how many and what type of shots you'll need next, and they'll direct you to their favorite photographers. In some cases, they can even help you get photos for reduced rates, at the photographer's cost, or even free.

FINDING A PHOTOGRAPHER

You'll need to find a photographer who specializes in model's portfolios or commercial work—not school pictures, not wedding pictures, and not animal portraits. You can begin your search by calling the talent and modeling agencies that you intend to eventually approach and asking them to recommend some names to you. Some will just give you one or two names; others will send you a huge list with thirty to forty studios on it. Once you have your recommendations, get on the phone and do some calling. Ask for prices, specialties (some photographers prefer fashion, while others are better at character model and actor's resume type shots). Find out if there are any hidden extra costs; for instance, some photographer's will only shoot you if you use a certain makeup artist, and this adds to your expense.

Don't be surprised if the prices vary greatly from photographer to photographer; those who are well known through their commercial work or have a large studio and staff at an expensive address will charge more than a photographer who has a smaller studio (or even shoots out of his home) or who is less well known. But roughly, you can expect to pay $70 to $120 per 36-exposure roll. This price usually doesn't include a stylist (to prop and accessorize) or a makeup artist.

Once you've gleaned your information over the phone, narrow down the field to three or four choices based on price, location, and any other factors pertinent to you. Call this handful of photographers back to ask for an appointment to meet, to look at their work, and to ask additional questions.

When you meet the photographer, remember that your purpose is not just to examine his work, but to see how comfortable you feel with him, as well. Photographers are human beings, of course, with personal style and quirks just like anyone else. No matter how established or technically expert a photographer is, if you don't feel comfortable with him, you won't have a successful photo session. This is no one's fault, it's simply a fact of life.

So be aware of how well the two of you interact when you're looking at his work. And don't be razzle-dazzled by a lot of commercial work; pay more attention to the work that actually pertains to you—his samples of model's portfolio shots. Look especially for good, solid examples of MOR head shots with pleasant expressions, relaxed poses, and flattering lighting, since this is the type of shot you'll be getting first.

Be sure to ask all pertinent questions you can think of at this meeting. The more information on which you can base your choice of photographer, the happier you'll be with your final decision. To help you out in this area, copy the following list of questions and bring it to all your visits with photographers.

Photographer Information

1. What is the price per 36-exposure, b&w roll?

2. Does this price include a contact sheet and prints?

3. What is the price per 8 × 10, glossy, b&w print?

4. What is the price per hour for stylist?

5. What is the price per hour for makeup artist?

6. If you choose to forgo the services of a stylist and makeup artist, will the photographer advise you about props and accessories? Will he spot-check your makeup and hair for you at the time of the shoot?

7. What locations are available to you for full-body shots, and is there an extra charge for going on location?

8. Who owns the negatives? (Many photographers retain negatives for artistic control.)

You may also ask the photographer for suggestions about your most promising looks and market (does he see you as fashion, young parent, or business person?) and for suggestions about locations, situations, props, etc.

After you have been to several studios and gathered all your information, choose your photographer based on price, quality of work, and personality.

Once you've made your choice, take a look at his price list and juxtapose your photographic needs and budget with his prices to determine which type of shots and how many you will have taken at your first session. As I mentioned, most photographers charge by the 36-

One option for a character model who wants to start building a portfolio is a series of studio head shots featuring different expressions. Here we have: surprise . . .

. . . weariness . . .

. . . and delight!

exposure roll when shooting 35mm, and by the 12-exposure roll when shooting 2¼ format. You should use a full roll for each type of shot, or setup. Don't try to squeeze head shots and body shots all onto one roll. For most of us, it takes all twelve to thirty-six exposures to get one or two dynamite pictures. Your photographer might offer reduced rates on each additional roll after the first one; for example, he might charge $70 for the first roll and $45 each for additional rolls. If this is the case with the photographer you choose and you know you'll be needing a body shot, business shot, or character shot eventually, you may want to opt for two rolls. Otherwise, if the charge is the same per roll, you have nothing to lose by waiting to shoot the second roll until you've gotten some feedback from an agent.

Some photographers also offer packages called "portfolio shoots" or "composite shoots," which offer a certain number of rolls (often including color) and a certain number of prints for a somewhat lower, fixed price.

This may seem like a good deal, and down the road, it may be. But for now, when you're just starting out, one head shot and one body or character shot is plenty. Agents will not be dazzled by a huge quantity of photos. Especially now, when you're still just testing the water, quality is everything.

BOOKING YOUR SHOOT

Once you've chosen your photographer and determined your photographic needs, you can book your shoot.

Be sure to allow yourself time to prepare yourself psychologically and practice the hairstyling, makeup, and wardrobe you'll be using for the photo session.

Try to choose a day when you know you'll be well-rested. The day after cramming for a big test or attending a wild party is no good. Also, try to book the session for a time when your energy is highest. Morning people should shoot in the morning, and if you're one of those whose heart doesn't start beating until the P.M. hours, book in the afternoon. And choose a time when you won't be hassled. If you rush to your shoot after a long day at work and you have to rush away immediately afterward to pick up the kids at day care, you won't be at your best.

Of course, you won't be able to be this picky about professional jobs; when they want you to shoot, you just have to be there. But it doesn't hurt to give yourself every advantage when you're just starting out.

The Bottom Line These are the main things to remember when planning for your first professional photos:

1. Shop around and find the best photographer for the money and one with whom you feel comfortable. Price, quality, and style vary drastically.

2. Ask a lot of questions. You will need as much information as possible to choose a photographer and to determine the best way to fill your photographic needs within your budget.

3. Be prepared for your shoot. Book in advance with plenty of time to plan and try your wardrobe, hairstyle, and makeup. Also leave time to hunt down accessories.

An industrial/character model can start with two basic shots: an introductory head shot . . .

. . . and a location "reaction" shot that shows great expressiveness.

This is a good photo start for a male fashion model: a basic head shot . . .

. . . and a body shot that highlights his physique.

Sometimes a photographer will waive his fee, in return for your modeling services, for one photo session. This is called a "test" shoot. A test shoot is just what the name implies: it's a chance for the photographer to try out new ideas and techniques. Sometimes the results are good, sometimes bad, and often, very unusual and off-beat. These two examples are from test shoots.

The First Step—Photos

FIFTEEN

YOUR FIRST PHOTO SHOOT

Pretend it's your big day, the day of your first professional photo shoot. You did your homework and found a photographer you really like and trust. You've planned your wardrobe, hair, makeup, and accessories, and you've put it all together at home so you know it looks great. You won't be fighting your hair or makeup into a style you've never tried until five minutes before the session. You know where the studio is and how to get there. You've pored over magazines for posing ideas and have practiced in the mirror. You're abreast of all the fashion trends as well as the demands of your particular market. You've shot a few snaps with friends using b&w film, so you know how your tones are going to photograph. You're prepared down to the very last detail!

So why is your mouth dry and your heart in your throat? "You never grow out of a certain amount of nervousness before a shoot, whether it's for your portfolio or a paying job," said a nine-year modeling veteran, "but by far the two most nerve-wracking experiences the new model has to face are the *first* portfolio shoot, and the *first* paid job. It's the unknown, and it's really scary."

Under normal circumstances, it can take even an established model a whole roll of film to get one really great shot. A first-timer has to deal with inexperience coupled with nervousness, so the odds can be even worse. For this reason, some modeling school instructors and agents consider the first shoot a practice session, or a "throw away," because they know that successive shoots will yield much better results. If the first photo session does result in one or two good shots, they count the model lucky.

As a photographer shooting new and inexperienced

models, I suddenly realized what my dentist must have felt like whenever I walked into his office with an expression on my face that said, "Please hurt me and get it over with." It's hard to look attractive in photos when you're grimacing. But it doesn't have to be that way.

You see, many of the models I interviewed agreed that their first photo sessions would have been less unnerving if they could have had a mentor, a more experienced model who would relate stories about her own first shoot and offer advice. You may not have a friend who's able to do this for you, but this chapter will do the next best thing. It relates the stories of five experienced models and their earliest shoots. It tells you how they felt and what went on, and it gives you sound advice, based on their experiences, that you can use to make your own debut modeling for the camera a happy one. If you combine their advice with the relaxation methods at the end of this chapter, you will be able to trick any photographer into thinking you're an old pro.

Lynette: "Remember Who's Paying" "I was very intimidated by the photographer at my first portfolio shoot. He was very big; he shot national ads and he really only did portfolios for bread and butter. I figured he was this hotshot professional and I was nobody. So when I got to his studio there were about six other models waiting to be shot ahead of me. I had to wait forty-five minutes after my booked time to shoot. Then he sat me down in front of the camera and proceeded to pop off thirty-six shots in less than ten minutes, giving me no feedback at all and rushing me out so he could get to his next person. I didn't complain because I figured he was the professional, and that's the

ng the relaxation techniques outlined
his chapter can keep you from making
e common mistakes, like those shown

DON'T *pose with the face turned too
away from the camera.*

▲ DO *Relax! When you're relaxed,
your body flows naturally into fluid poses,
and your expression looks comfortable.*

◀ DON'T *lean too much toward the
camera with the neck, or force a broad,
unnatural smile.*

Your First Photo Shoot

▲ DON'T *If you're nervous, you might forget even the most elementary posing rules, such as not covering your face with your hand.*

▲ DO *But if you're calm, you will remember to direct the pinky edge of your hand toward the camera, and keep the hand from distorting or covering your face.*

way it was supposed to work. When I got my contact sheet, it looked like thirty-six of the identical shot, and not one was usable. Again I thought it was just because of my own inexperience. But I had forgotten one very important fact: I was paying him for that shoot. He was, in a way, my employee. I was buying his professional know-how and savvy. His responsibility was not just to click the camera; it was to give me the best shots he could. If I could have realized that going into the photo session, I would have demanded some feedback from him. And I would have asked him to slow down and shoot at a nicer pace.

"I'm sure my experience wasn't typical; I've worked with a lot of really great photographers since then. But even if you're shooting for the first time with a photographer you really like and trust, it can still help to remember that for that one roll of film, those thirty-six shots, he is your employee. You are paying him."

Barbara: "It's Not Just a Lark"
"I tried to use reverse psychology on myself for my first shoot. I figured that if I pretended it didn't mean anything to me, then I wouldn't be nervous when the time came. So I did nothing to prepare myself. I thought, 'Oh, it'll just fall together on the day of the shoot.' Well, I was just kidding myself. That shoot meant a lot to me or I wouldn't have booked it in the first place. My casual attitude brought me to the studio totally unprepared, and just as terrified! I had forgotten my under eye cover-up. When I put on the off-the-shoulder dress I had chosen for my head shot, I discovered that the tan marks from my recent trip to Mexico virtually glowed. I had the wrong color hose for the full-length photo, and a horrified look on my face in every shot. The photographer was really sweet about it and tried to joke me out of it. He offered to reschedule me for a 'more convenient time,' but for some reason I felt I had to go through with it right then and there. All this because I thought I could fool myself into thinking it was just a lark. If I had been honest with myself and admitted it was something I really wanted to do, and wanted to do well, I would've been prepared. I might have gotten one or two good shots instead of seventy-two awful ones."

Anne: "Tell the Photographer How You Feel"
"I went to my first session determined that my photographer wouldn't know that I was a 'modeling virgin.' When he asked me if I'd had any experience, I just said, 'Oh, this and that.' I sat there in front of the camera so intent on looking 'cool' that I came off looking like death warmed over. That was for the first ten or so shots. Then all of a sudden, I don't know what hit me, but I leveled with him. I said, 'Boy, am I nervous! I've never done this before.' We both had a good laugh. He came up with a hundred reasons why I shouldn't be nervous. We stopped and talked a little.

Then when we started again, we got some pretty good shots."

Cindy: "Learn the Difference Between Inexperienced and Stupid"
"At my first time, I thought I was failing miserably. The photographer had to keep saying, 'Lower your chin. Lower your chin, please,' and I kept popping it up in the air like the Queen of Sheba. Finally, after he told me to lower my chin about ten times, I just blurted out, 'Oh, I'm so bad at this!' I thought I was really stupid for not being able to do what he asked me. Then he asked me if this was my first shoot, and I said it was. So he told me, 'Well, you're inexperienced, you're not bad. If you've never done it before, you can't expect to be perfect. I have to tell a lot of people to lower their chins.' Well, he was right. I was expecting myself to burst onto the modeling scene as good as girls who had been working for years at it. When I realized that inexperienced (and nervous!) was not the same as stupid or hopeless, I was able to do a lot better. And I kept my darned chin down."

Liz: "Know Your Strengths"
"Let me start out by telling you that I'm simply not fashion model material—although I am truly adorable, and I'll be the first to admit it—but for some reason I had this idea in my head that I had to be a fashion model or nothing. So I booked a shoot and showed up with sexy clothes and heavy makeup, and I tried to do all of these seductive, wet-lipped looks. The whole time I thought, 'This guy must think I'm totally out of my gourd.' The photos were awful; they looked like a farce on fashion modeling. But I was determined, so I took them into an agent. Luckily, she was creative and insightful enough to look past my lousy pictures and imagine what kind of modeling I'd really be good at. She told me straight out that I was an industrial, not a fashion model. She told me to get some "mommish" and business shots and come back, and she would register me. At first I was crushed. I refused to do it for eight months. But then I decided what the hell, it was better to be a character model than a waitress, so I had another shoot and got the right kind of pictures. That session was completely different from the first one. It wasn't uncomfortable; I felt attractive instead of silly; and the shots were great. If only I had come to terms with my strengths and weaknesses earlier, I would have saved myself a lot of time and embarrassment."

These models all cited things they wish they had known before they went into their first portfolio shoots, things they had to learn through experience. But now you have read their stories, and you have the extra advantage of their insights.

Now how can you help yourself cope with that first photo session? What should you think about during the

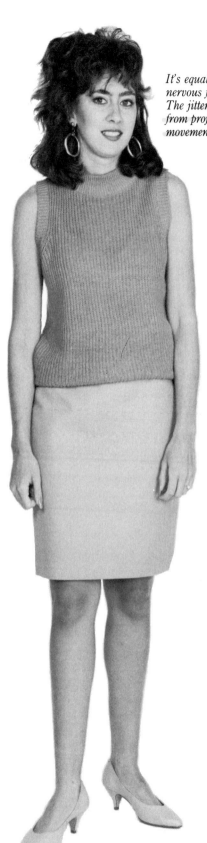

It's equally important not to be nervous for full-length shots. The jitters can hold you back from projecting energy and movement.

By relaxing and shifting her weight, this model added needed life and energy to her pose.

A calm person is more likely to remember to keep her movements from side to side . . .

. . . rather than making the mistake of directing her movement into the camera.

shoot? How can you develop a positive attitude toward the photographer and the camera itself?

RELAX

The single most important thing you have to do—and the most difficult—is to simply relax. A few very lucky people are perfectly at home in front of the camera, naturally. But if you're like most of us, learning to relax during a photo session will be an ongoing process that may last as long as your career. I've photographed seasoned actors, with performance histories of twenty-five years and longer, who would face the lens with the same spirit a child has when he faces a dentist's drill. Being photographed is a naturally tense situation. How do you overcome it? The following nine relaxation methods are used by professional models.

Breathe One of the major keys to relaxation is breathing. Yes, in a state of panic we can even forget the most basic functions. We all react differently under stress: some of us hyperventilate, and some of us hold our breath. Both can cause tight-chested, dizzy sensations. In either case, this simple breathing exercise can help:

Close your eyes and count slowly to thirty while imagining yourself in a peaceful place such as a pasture or an island. Become aware of how you are breathing. Then inhale to a slow count of four; exhale from four to one; inhale from one to four, and so on. Place your hand on your diaphragm and concentrate on expanding your entire chest from the bottom, rather than taking shallow breaths that only partially expand your lungs. As you regain control of your breathing, you should feel yourself relaxing.

Surroundings Another relaxation aid is to become familiar with your surroundings. Arrive for your shoot a few minutes early. Look around the studio and familiarize yourself with the equipment. As the photographer is loading his camera and preparing for the shoot, ask questions about where the light will be coming from and about anything else that comes to your mind. Most photographers are more than willing to talk shop. However, you should only do this at a portfolio shoot; on a paid job you're required to stay out of the way until needed.

Trust You must trust the photographer, and even the camera itself, in order to relax. How do you think of them? Do you see the photographer as an adversary, someone who's eagerly waiting for a chance to catch you at a bad angle or who will compare you to other, more beautiful models? Do you see the camera as a

cold, mechanical eyeball focused on your worst features? If these thoughts have passed through your mind even fleetingly, then you really need to work on your attitude. Let's look at it logically. The photographer wants you to look great as much as you do; it's simply not in his best interests to have one of his clients running around town showing people samples of his work that are bad. As for judging your appearance, photographers, more than anyone else (except maybe your own mother), can perceive the attractiveness in your face. They have to so they can bring it out in your photos. And while the camera, used carelessly, can sometimes emphasize certain facial flaws, used artfully it can be amazingly forgiving. So try to view the photographer and his camera as allies. After all, you're both working toward the same goal—beautiful pictures of you.

Concentrate You can also enhance your relaxation by losing yourself in the mechanics of the shoot. Concentrate on asking yourself questions. Where is the camera? Where is the main light source? Where is the light? If I turn my face away from the main light, will there be a shadow, or is there a reflector to pick it up on the other side?

Acting You could lose yourself by playing a character. This is easy if you're a character model portraying a businessperson or a housewife. Just make up a story in your mind about who you are: "I just landed a huge account and boy, am I happy!", or, "While I'm sitting here talking to you, I'm cleaning my oven!" This technique can work for fashion models, as well. Determine the mood or quality you're trying to project—friendly, sophisticated, vulnerable, sexy—and *act* it. Think of someone who embodies that quality and be her: Mata Hari, Sophia Loren, a lost child. By being someone else, you can forget your nervousness.

Imagining Some people tell me they like to use their imaginations to project themselves into a different place or situation during a photo session. One woman pretended the camera was her husband and she was having dinner with him at their favorite restaurant. Another model sometimes likes to imagine he's on a cruise ship, looking into the lens as though he's looking at the ocean.

Shake it Out If necessary, you can literally shake out the tension. Take a moment to roll your neck and shoulders. Shake your hands, arms, and torso. Don't worry about looking silly; the photographer has seen it all before!

Listen Many models forget their anxiety when they concentrate on anticipating the needs of the photographer

▲ DO *Use your environment (in this case, the pole) to create poses on location.*

▲ DON'T *try to hide!*

and responding to his instructions. Focus your whole attention and intent on doing what he asks of you.

Be in the Present Live the photo session one moment at a time. Some of us try to predict how every shot will look as a finished print before the shutter clicks, hoping each one will be "it." That can be terrifying. Take the session one shot at a time, and never try to predict the outcome. Don't second-guess yourself by wondering, "Was that a good enough smile? I'll bet my bad tooth was showing on that last one." Keep your mind in the present moment.

Not all of these techniques work for everyone. You'll need to experiment to find out which ones really help you, and then be sure to always practice them.

SIXTEEN

PICKING YOUR PICS

Within a week or two weeks after your photo shoot, you should receive your contact sheets. A contact sheet is a sheet of photo paper on which the negative strips are laid out and exposed to light. When it's developed, all thirty-six exposures (exactly the same size as their negatives) are on the one 8 × 10 sheet, with the negative numbers to the right of each tiny print. See the photo. You use the miniatures on this sheet to help you determine which shots to have printed as 8 × 10 or 11 × 14 finished pictures for your portfolio or composite.

Most newcomers to modeling have never seen so many shots of themselves in one place before. The experience can be overwhelming. I've heard people react to their contact sheets in a variety of ways—everything from "These are wonderful!" to "Yuck. Is that what I really look like? I hate my nose."

It usually takes a couple of days of looking at the contact sheets for people to come around to a realistic view of their photos and to be able to see past their real and imagined attributes and flaws to the overall effect of the shots. Most of us have to work hard at learning to look at photos of ourselves objectively and, even then, we're probably still our own worst critics. After all, you're more sensitive to your flaws. When you're just starting out, you might not know what the demands of your market are and you'll tend to pick a shot that hides your irregularities (perhaps at the cost of honestly representing yourself) over a shot that's overall commercially successful. The image you have of yourself may not be your best or most salable look, i.e., you may choose a sultry-looking shot when an all-American-looking one will suit you better.

GENERAL RULES FOR PICKING YOUR PICS

How can you learn to be a better judge of which shots should be made into prints? Are there any guidelines for how to choose the most attractive and marketable photos?

1. Always sleep on it—never decide on the spur of the moment. Your first impression is rarely a lasting one when it comes to your own face.

2. If possible, always consult with an agent when choosing which shots to print. An agent will be more objective; she's a professional who knows her market better than anyone else possibly could.

3. View the contact sheet several times a day for at least two or three days. Each time you look at it, use a grease pencil to indicate the ones that catch your eye and to help you narrow the field. Mark the ones that others have liked, as well. (Use different marks for yourself, your agent, your friends, and so on.) If you change your mind, you can scrape marks off with your fingernail.

4. Buy a magnifying loupe, a glass that makes the contact prints seem bigger to the eye and can help you get a better idea of what the final print will look like. A loupe may draw your attention to details that seem inconsequential to the naked eye. Glare, a shadow, a stray hair in the eyes, a missing button, or slightly droopy eyelids may make the difference between a good and a bad shot.

5. Cut a square out of the center of a blank piece of paper or cardboard approximately 1″ × 1 ¼″ in size; this is proportionate to the dimensions of an 8 × 10 print, and it will help you get a better idea of what the composition of the

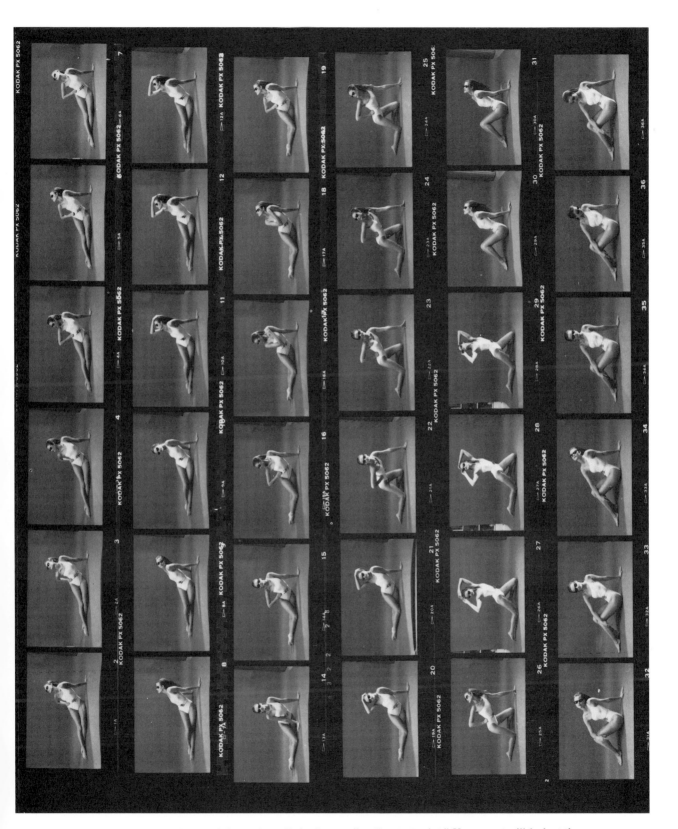

This is an example of a proof sheet, also called a "contact" or "contact print." Your agent will look at the proof sheet with you through a magnifying glass or loupe, and help you choose which shots to blow up into 8x10 finished prints to be used in your portfolio and on your composite photo.

photo will be like once it's blown up. It can also help you decide whether a certain photo needs special cropping.

6. If you have trouble imagining what the shot will look like from sliding the cutout over it, try simply blocking in the cropping that you prefer with a china marker or grease pencil.

7. Ask for feedback from your mother, spouse, friends, and others, but take it with a grain of salt. Everyone to whom you are important has different ideas and expectations about how they want you to look, and they probably don't have any idea what kind of looks are marketable in your city. However, listening to their ideas about the positive and negative things they see in each photo may help you look at the shots with a fresh perspective.

8. Try to put yourself in the shoes of the clients, those you hope will offer you modeling work on the basis of your photos. If you owned a company that sold casual clothing, how would you want a model to look in one of your advertisements? What if you owned a company that sold medical supplies or wallpaper?

9. If possible, go to an agency or a printer who specializes in models' composites and look at several hundred photos. Try to analyze what each of them has in common. Compare them to your own photos. Which of your own shots has the same qualities or mood as the best of the other models' shots you looked at?

WHAT TO LOOK FOR

Sometimes the difference between a good photo and a great photo seems totally intangible. There are, however, some very concrete elements you should look for when choosing which photos to have printed.

1. A comfortable and logical pose that fits the wardrobe, facial expression, lighting, and overall mood of the shot. Whether a pose is editorial or catalog style, it should never look forced or incongruous.

2. A facial expression that seems natural—not as though you're trying too hard, but not too understated, either.

3. Visual interest, good contrast, good line or movement in the composition, and some texture.

4. The energy level should be high, even in pensive or moody shots.

5. For shots in which the model is looking into the camera, there must be excellent eye contact; the eyes should not look dreamy, unfocused, or vague. For shots in which the model is looking away from the lens, her eye must be positioned so that her iris is sufficiently apparent or her eyeball will look entirely white—a kind of "exorcist" effect. In order to achieve good eye position, sometimes the model

has to "fudge" and focus her eyes on a spot that is closer to the camera than she would if she were really looking in the direction that her head position indicates.

6. The camera emphasizes all imperfections. If a flaw is apparent on the contact sheet, you can bet it will look three times as bad on the final print. There should be no stains, sweater snags, missing buttons, wild hairs, unnatural or overt wrinkles in the clothing, or smudged makeup. Resist the urge to print up a shot that contains this type of imperfection; even if the pose, lighting, and facial expression are excellent, the eye will be drawn to the out-of-place detail first. If there's a shot you are absolutely enthralled with, ask your photographer if there's anything he can do about the flaw. Hairs, dark wrinkles, and shadows usually can't be touched out, but stains and other minor distractions can sometimes be eliminated with retouching.

7. When choosing which pictures to have blown up into prints, always juxtapose them with the shots you've already got, if any. For instance, if you already have a smiling, pretty MOR head shot, you may want to choose a different expression from your next contact sheet, perhaps a shot with a more serious or sultry mood. If you already have an active body shot, say one that shows you running through water in a bathing suit or playing tennis in a tank top and shorts, you may want to go for a more sedate and sophisticated pose from your next batch of shots, perhaps a pose in an evening dress.

If it's financially feasible for you, it can be beneficial to narrow your choices down to two favorite shots per setup and have them both printed before you decide which of them to use on your composite or in your portfolio. Even after having made thousands of prints, I'm still surprised occasionally by the way an 8 × 10 can look very different from its contact print.

What should you do if you and your agent disagree on which shot or shots to print? I recommend using the agent's choice for your portfolio and getting a print of the one that you like for personal use. Some models have the attitude, "Well, it's my print, my portfolio, and my money; I have to live with it, so I'll pick the one I want." This may be true, but it's not that simple an issue. If you allow your agent to choose your promotional material for you, you may have a more lucrative modeling career.

And there's one more good reason to let your agent have the final say in choosing your prints for you. Your promotional material reflects on her and her agency. If she's not happy with the prints you choose to include in your composite and portfolio, she'll be less likely to send them out to clients. But if she's happy with your photos, which is more likely if you let her choose them, she'll probably promote you much harder.

SEVENTEEN

YOUR PORTFOLIO

Your portfolio, or *book*, is the case of photos you'll bring with you to auditions and interviews with clients, runway coordinators, casting directors, and anyone else who might give you a modeling job. Like your composite, your portfolio should show your moods; your complete age range; and a full variety of looks, hairstyles, and characters. But unlike the composite, which must put across your complete versatility with just four or five shots, you may have room in your portfolio to expand and take the luxury of many more photos to express yourself.

In addition to photos and tear sheets, you might want to include color slides, color Xerox copies made from color slides, 4 × 5 color transparencies, color prints, and b&w and color contact sheets from a particularly good shoot (some clients like to see contacts to find out what percentage of shots are keepers from your sessions).

How many photos should you include in your portfolio, and what types? Everyone's book is different. You need to custom build your portfolio according to your financial means, your market, your look, your special talents, and your agent's preferences.

Most agents I interviewed suggested having twelve to sixteen good shots in your portfolio. "Any less, and you seem too 'green.' Any more, and the client may get too overwhelmed flipping page after page. With all those shots to look at, nothing in particular will stick out in his mind after you leave," explained an agent. I've seen models with portfolios that made very effective presentations with as few as ten or as many as thirty-five shots and tear sheets.

RATIO OF COLOR TO B&W

Some agents like the fashion models they represent to have up to 50 percent color shots in their books. Other agents think one or two really good color shots are enough. In my own experience, it's much more cost-effective to get plenty of good, marketable b&w photos first, and then to add some color shots after you've had one or two modeling jobs and made back part of your initial investment. Of course if you're lucky enough to get a photo test, you won't have any choice as to whether the shots are color or b&w, but either will be equally advantageous to you.

Again, the type of shots you have in your portfolio will vary according to many factors. But there are some very general guidelines to follow when compiling your book. Here are some suggestions you can refer to as you plan your photo sessions. Use them as a reference point, but you don't have to follow them to the letter.

Major Components of a Fashion Portfolio

1. MOR introductory head shot.

2. Body shot. Preferably have it taken on location at a gym; a lake; a marina; a pool; or anywhere else you might wear a leotard, swimwear, or active wear. If you have this shot taken in the studio against seamless paper, use simple props to enhance the composition.

3. Elegant evening fashion shot. Again, having the shot taken on location is ideal, perhaps on the steps or beside the pillars outside of a museum or theater, or maybe on a city street at dusk. Sit down with your photographer and brainstorm. If you do this shot in the studio it can be enhanced with dramatic lighting, unusual angles, or a textured backdrop.

4. Sporty, casual, catalog-type shot. Wear tennis clothes, a neat blouse and slacks, or a sweater and skirt—something you might actually see advertised in a real catalog. The pose should be casual and natural, the energy high. You should be smiling and looking directly into the lens.

5. High fashion head shot. The makeup is more dramatic than for the MOR head shot, and the hairstyle should be dressier. The facial expression and overall mood can be more serious or sultry. And unlike the MOR head shot, it's OK to accessorize dramatically. Wear a huge pair of earrings, a hat, a veil, hair ornaments, chunky bracelets, or necklaces.

6. Three-quarter-length to waist-length business shot. This shot is to cultivate work in nonfashion areas. Again, shooting on location is ideal. Downplay your makeup (the less glamorous, the better for this look) and wear your hair in a style that looks conservative and neat.

7. Three-quarter-to full-length shot with another model. This shot should be in your most marketable category, which is catalog fashion for most of us. It features you with another model, of the same or opposite sex, to show that you can work well as a team member.

8. Head shot, possibly color, with yet another hairstyle and expression. Take into consideration your strengths and personal tastes for this one. Like the urban look? Try shooting in denim with new wave hair. Like country? Try a soft, wavy hairstyle with a western hat and top.

For your remaining shots, concentrate on more variations of your most marketable looks. If you're having trouble coming up with ideas, talk to your agent and to a photographer or two. I can guarantee they'll have opinions!

To see how we put a portfolio together for Lysa, a young fashion model, look at the photos.

Major Components of a Character Model's Portfolio The standards and requirements for a character model's portfolio aren't as defined as they are for a fashion model's, and they tend to vary from agent to agent and city to city. Generally character models do not need any color shots in their books. Some agents like to have their character models shoot a portion of their books on location like fashion models do. Others like the shots to be done in the studio with or without simple props. It's very important to check with your agent to find out what kinds of shots she requires before you spend a lot of money. If you haven't got an agent, your photographer will probably have a pretty good idea of what types of shots will get you the farthest in your community. The following is a list of shots that covers all the bases, so no matter what your market or your agent's preferences, there's something for everyone.

1. Introductory or resume head shot. Like an MOR introductory fashion shot, it should show your teeth, ears, and full face. It should be shot with studio lighting, a simple background, and minimal accessories.

2. Full-length or three-quarter business shot, preferably on location.

3. Family shot. Are you a young parent, an older parent or a grandparent? This shot should be taken on location with a child the appropriate age in a park playing ball, in a restaurant, or in another place where a parent or grandparent might spend time with a child. If you can't find a child, have the shot taken in a grocery store, a laundry room, or another location that implies that you have a family.

4. Character shot from one of your area's most marketable industries. You could be a doctor, a dentist, a cab driver, etc. How you portray this person will depend on whether you're the pleasant, average type or a broader character. Go with your special talents.

5. Contrasting industry shot. If you did a doctor for your first shot, do a dock worker or a greenhorn business type for this one to emphasize versatility.

6. Three or four reaction shots. Have these taken in the studio. You should be framed from the waist up using a simple prop like a coffee cup, a baby blanket, money, a bill, or anything you can imagine that would give you an excuse to mug for the camera.

Flesh out your book according to your needs from there. To see how my husband and I put together a portfolio for Vivian, look at the photos.

PRESENTATION

How should you arrange and present your photos, once you've got them? Some people prefer to place all the highly marketable shots, such as the MOR head shot and catalog body shots, in the front of the book and end with the editorial and "artsy" shots. Some like to begin with all head shots, then three-quarter, then full-length. I like to see contrasting shots on pages facing each other, because it displays your versatility to greatest advantage. This is how Lysa's and Vivian's shots are arranged.

As you show your book to various agents and clients, take note of the responses you get to the different shots. Pick out the two shots that seem to get the most positive feedback. Place one at the beginning and one at the back of your portfolio, so you can begin and end it with a bang!

When you go to an audition, you already have one foot in the door. Use your portfolio to get you the rest of the way in. Make it speak for you.

This basic head shot is a good choice to start Lysa's book. She uses minimal makeup and no accessories to distract from her fresh, natural, youthful look.

This body shot elegantly shows off Lysa's beautiful figure without looking cheap or "cheesecake."

This head shot is a more dramatic, moodier look, to complement the fresh quality of her basic head shot.

This shot shows how her fresh, friendly look is great for catalog work.

Here, Lysa's sophisticated side comes out.

This playful,
rustic look is
a natural for Lysa.

This aloof, editorial shot contrasts with the warm, smiling
balloon shot (page 134), emphasizing her versatility.

This urban look was shot on a
fire escape with natural lighting
emphasizing her strong cheekbones and jaw.

Lysa's complexion really shines in this headshot. Her playful expression and pose add interest, too.

*Shot at an old-fashioned drive-in restaurant, this shot
further rounds out a young fashion model's portfolio.*

Vivian is an industrial print model who also does live runway fashion. Her portfolio begins with a basic introductory shot.

Naturally, a business shot is a must for all mature models, male and female.

Since Vivian also does fashion modeling, we had included a three-quarter fashion body shot.

This shot, taken at an outdoor cafe, reflects the trend in advertising of depicting mature consumers as happy, active people who are enjoying life.

This sporty shot shows Vivian's slender figure and contrasts well with her fashion and business looks.

An elegant head shot finishes Vivian's book. She will fill her book further with tearsheets from actual ads as she continues to work as a print model.

EIGHTEEN

YOUR COMPOSITE PHOTO

A composite photo, or *comp,* is one sheet of high quality, stiff paper, usually 8×10 or 5×8 with two to five photos of you printed on one or both sides, along with your applicable statistics, or *stats.* The types of photos, how many, and which stats you should include on your comp vary depending on whether you're a fashion model, character model, or both and what your strengths and weaknesses are.

Your comp is your single most important promotional tool. It introduces you to potential clients and, ideally, it shows them many things about you:

1. Your face. The shots should show your face in the most flattering and straightforward way, without dramatic or contrasty lighting, background, or accessories. You want your head shot to show you in the most favorable manner possible, but it should also be a true representation of what you look like. "You don't want to show up for an audition and have the client say, 'But we thought you were fifteen years younger,' " said a model.

2. Your hairstyle. Wear it as you do most of the time (preferably down, rather than in a bun or a ponytail) so its length and style are apparent. Include some variations to show different looks.

3. Your ability to strike attractive poses and express a feeling that complements the other elements of the photographs.

4. Your camera presence. This is the quality you have that comes across in every shot, whether you're projecting a dramatic mood or a comic one. It's an energy or charisma that's similar to an actor's stage presence.

5. Your level of experience. Sometimes the client can extrapolate how much modeling experience you've had by how many different photographers' work appears on your comp, whether there are any tear sheets included, and whether the shots show variety in style and background.

6. Your versatility. Your shots should show you are versatile in looks, moods, and poses. That's why it's very important not to include shots on your comp that are similar in any way. The wardrobe, facial expressions, angles, poses, lighting, hair, makeup should be different in every shot.

7. Your body type. Your height, weight, and build should be apparent in at least one of the photos or from the stats included on your comp.

8. Your age range. This should also be apparent from the comp. If you can do a teenager as well as you can do a mature businessperson, show it. The client won't know all the different roles he could potentially cast you in unless you show him.

Of course, in order to put all of these different elements across to your best advantage, your composite needs to be carefully planned and executed.

WHEN YOU SHOULD GET A COMP

The agents I spoke with had varying opinions about when a model should have her first comp printed. Some agents won't promote a model until they have a comp from her, in which case she needs to put one together immediately. Others prefer to simply make a Xerox copy of a good head shot and use that to promote the model until she's had

This composite for a male industrial/character model includes the introductory head shot, a young father shot, a business shot, and the product shot with a coffee cup.

Your Composite Photo

some experience and has had the time to shoot with enough different photographers to put together a really diverse comp from paid jobs, tests, and portfolio shoots.

Whichever route they preferred, all the agents agreed that no one should rush to throw a comp together without sufficient planning and that a model should wait until she has a good number of shots to choose from. "I've seen people put together comps where all the shots were taken in the same dress, with the same lighting and expression. They just flushed their money down the toilet. The point is not just to have a comp, it's to have a good comp," said Julie, an agent.

So you should wait to make up your comp until you've got plenty of photos to choose from. Those who aren't lucky enough to get photo tests or paid jobs may have to wait until they can afford two or more photo sessions with recommended photographers before putting together a comp. While the costs of photographs and the printing of the composite itself may seem expensive, it is the most cost-effective way to reach clients in the long run.

HOW AND WHERE TO GET A COMP PRINTED

Some agencies put together a bound book containing the composite photos of all their talent, which they submit to all their clients and update every two to three years. Models who are represented by the agency can get their photos into the book for a fee, which usually includes the price of up to a thousand loose composites for use in self-promotion. The fee for being included in the book and receiving your loose comps through the agency is usually cheaper than going to a printer and having the comp made up on your own. The agencies that don't have a *book* refer models to a preferred printer to have their comps made up.

Whether you go through an agent or take your photos to a printer independently, you can expect to pay between $150 and $250 for your first year's supply of composites (about one hundred to five hundred copies).

You don't need the negatives to get your composite printed; there are two different printing methods used for comp photos, and they are both reproduced from 8×10 prints. The first method is photographic reproduction. Negatives are made from the original prints in exactly the size they will appear on the comp. These negatives are pasted together and the stats are printed in. Then the composite photo is printed on photographic paper from this composite negative. This process can cost anywhere from $60 per hundred copies for a simple resume head shot with the name typeset at the bottom to $110 for a comp with up to five shots on it.

The second method is called screening. The original prints are reduced, and the images are translated into dots by a graphic arts, or *photostat,* camera. The composite can then be pasted together and printed by normal offset printing methods on ordinary paper. The quality and cost of this type of printing varies greatly, according to the type of plate (metal or paper) and the coarseness of the screen, so be sure to do comparative shopping and learn as much as you can about this process before investing in your comp.

The typeface and layout are generally chosen and executed by the printer, as well.

Your agent probably has a standard format for comps that she encourages all her talent to use; discuss this with her before you go to the printer. Also find out whether your agent prefers matte or glossy paper. If you're using a printer who works closely with your agency, he'll probably already know what type of format and paper your agent prefers.

If you're putting together a composite photo without the aid of an agent, try to get other models' comps and ask the printer to lay yours out similar to the most successful ones.

Color Some models use 5×8, two-sided composites and run a color photo on one side and two or three black and white photos on the other. They reason that the spot of color will draw attention to their comp and make it stand out. This may have some validity, but most agents will tell you that using color on your comp is unnecessary and extremely costly. "I don't even like my people to use it because it's very expensive, and the quality of the color reproduction is often very, very poor," said Andrea, an agent. "I'd rather see them spend the money on another photo shoot for some good b&w prints. They can save the color shots for their portfolios."

STATS

What statistics should you include on your composite? For fashion models: name, height, weight, hair color, eye color, sizes (dress, slacks, and blouse) or measurements (bust, waist, and hip) and shoe size. The stats on a typical fashion model's comp might run like this:
Jane Doe

Height: 5'9"

Weight: 120

Hair: Honey Blonde

Eyes: Brown

Bust: 34

Waist: 24

Hips: 35

Shoes: 8½

or Dress: 8

Pants: 8

Blouse: 6

For a male character model, the stats might run something like this:
John Smith

Height: 6'

Weight: 185

Eyes: Brown

Hair: Gray

Suit: 44L

Shirt: 17x34

Slacks: 34/36

Shoes: 11

Hat: 7¼

There's no need for the male character model to adhere to the size 40R restriction that fashion models use as a rule of thumb. Your comp should include any specialties, for instance, "excellent hands," at the bottom of the comp. Never include the date the comp was made or your birth date.

PHOTOS

How many and what types of photos should you include on your comp? Again, you should check with your agent since different agents have different preferences, but there are some general, common sense rules that are followed when choosing photos for a comp.

A Fashion Model's Picture Composite

1. An MOR head shot

2. A contrasting head shot, perhaps young mom or high fashion looks

3. A body shot in swimwear or a leotard

4. A location business shot or, for an alternative to the business shot if you're only concerned with pursuing fashion work and evening wear, a full-length body shot.

Character Model's 4-Picture Composite

1. An MOR head shot

2. A three-quarter body business shot

3. A family type shot (young parent or grandparent)

4. A shot pertaining to a marketable industry (dentistry, pharmaceutical, medical, etc.)

Or a character model's composite can be a series of four head shots featuring various expressions or reactions. These may be shot in the studio and may include simple props (coffee cup, briefcase, books, and so on). "I like my people to use this format if they've got extremely expressive faces; that's what we're selling, after all. They don't need a full body shot if they're characters; the client can judge their body build well enough from their stats," said an agent.

Is it acceptable to use photographs that were all taken by the same photographer in the same photo session? The agents' responses were mixed. "That's fine, as long as they're good shots with good lighting and locations and with wardrobe and makeup changes," said Mary. But another agent said, "I prefer for my people to shoot with at least two different photographers for their comps. It makes them look more established and gives them better experience."

So the last word is: Planning! Work with an agent if you have one. If you don't, do lots of research and find out as much as you can before investing your money. Construct your composite carefully; if it expresses your full range of talent and versatility, it will be your biggest asset in your pursuit of a modeling career.

NINETEEN

AGENCIES

Throughout this book, the words *agent* and *talent agent* crop up again and again. You've been told to try to please your agent with appropriate photos and accept your agent's guidance even if it's contrary to your self-image or your initial goals as an aspiring model. Why?

WHAT DO AGENTS DO?
Why do you need an agent, and what does one do for you besides take 15 percent of your earnings? The answer is—plenty!

Set Billing Rates Since there is no union for print models, the agents set the standard for billing rates. The agencies see that the models receive the highest rate of pay possible. Models who freelance—by choice or by necessity—often earn much lower rates than models who are represented by an agency.

Negotiate Unfixed Rates Rates of pay for regular print modeling and some other types of modeling are fixed to an extent. The model receives a regular hourly rate, but the rate is established by the agent and can vary more than fifty dollars per hour within any given market. Rates for certain other types of work, such as billboard or lingerie modeling, are unfixed, though, and can be negotiated by the agent to your best advantage. If you were forced to do your own negotiation, chances are you wouldn't fare nearly as well.

Screening Clients Most agencies run a credit check on prospective clients before booking talent for them. Clients with histories of not paying their bills or of paying too slow-

ly are eliminated, thus protecting the model from those with unscrupulous business practices.

Protecting Clients The agency not only protects models; it also protects clients. A photography coordinator for a huge department store said, "I book all my talent through one agency. I know the models I get through them will be prompt, prepared, and will know their stuff. It's too much of a risk to hire a freelancer; and anyway, it's unprofessional. If there's a model I'm interested in using but she's not listed with an agency, I tell her to go list with the one I book through, and then I'll use her. But I don't book anyone unless it's through an agency."

So the talent agent protects the client from flighty and unprofessional models, in effect funneling the trustworthy clients to the trustworthy models.

Client Services The agency also provides countless other benefits and services to the client that make it worth his while to pay the higher booking fees the agency charges. For instance, say a clothing store wanted to hold a cattle call to cast a Sunday ad. That client, working without the aid of an agent, would have to get the names and phone numbers of fifty to one hundred models and call to schedule all of them himself. Then, after the cattle call, say he's chosen ten models to appear in the ad; he'd have to call each one, tell her what clothes and accessories to bring to the shoot, schedule the shoot, and then send out ten different checks to ten different addresses. But if he works through an agent, she does all that work for him, and he sends out only one check. The agent also gives the client input, suggesting certain models she thinks he might like to use for certain ads. She takes any complaints the client has about her models and does her best to see the problems don't happen again, so that the client-model relationship will be a happy one for both parties.

Reputation When you're represented by a top-notch modeling agency, you immediately gain the privilege of basking in their reflected glory; their good name precedes you. Therefore, you, as a model affiliated with such an agency, seem more desirable to clients than you would as a freelancer, even with the same comps and portfolio, personality, and level of talent and experience.

Career Guidance When you register with an agency and begin to work with one of the agents, or *bookers*, you're receiving the benefit of all her years of expertise in the business, the years in business of the agency itself, and the bird's-eye perspective of someone involved in the very center of the industry—someone who intimately knows the market, the clients, and the models. She'll use her expertise to help you set and achieve realistic modeling goals. The advice of an agent can mean the difference between success and failure.

Business Friend Sometimes the role the agent plays in her models' lives becomes more personal. Lisa, a broadcast booker at the Eleanor Moore Agency in Minneapolis, said, "I know people's daily schedules and little details about their lives. Sometimes they confide in me. I look at myself as part private eye, part housemother, part matchmaker. I love people contact. I love to hear the happy voices over the phone when I call them and say, 'You got the job!'"

Promotion The agent also helps you compile promotional material, such as your comp and book. And she promotes you in her own material such as a fashion poster featuring all the agency's talent, which she distributes to clients. The agent teaches you to promote yourself, as well as doing some of your promotion for you. If you tried to start self-promoting without the benefit of the agent's client contacts—in other words, cold—you would be, in the words of one model who tried unsuccessfully to freelance in Minneapolis, "searching for a needle in a haystack; you just wouldn't know where to start."

You can probably understand now, after reading the extensive list of services the agent provides to both the model and the client, why her role is so important. She's certainly worth the 15 percent or so cut she takes from your pay rate, and to the client she's worth the higher rates she charges for your services.

FINDING AN AGENT

Now that we've established your need to be represented

by an agency, how do you go about finding one? How do you know if one is legitimate or disreputable?

Ask models or people involved in advertising and related fields for recommendations. If that fails, simply turn to your trusty yellow pages. Unfortunately, in many cities, modeling and talent agencies are listed on the same pages with escort services and firms specializing in more exotic forms of "talent." How can you tell which agencies to call?

Look for the agencies that are AFTRA affiliates. These are bound to be well-established and respected. As I mentioned in chapter five, beware of agencies that are involved with schools; frequently the agency is merely a listing service for the school, which doesn't really generate much employment for its models. If you approach one of these, you may wind up getting sold classes that you don't need and can't afford. If an agency that's affiliated with a school promises you modeling work if you finish one or more of their courses, don't believe them. No one can guarantee work.

There are other tip-offs that an agency is not legitimate. If they ask for a fee to list you, don't look back—just run the other way. Legitimate agencies may charge a fee for printing your head shot or composite within their promotional material, but this is always optional. They never charge a fee simply for representing you.

How to Approach Them Once you have found an agency, what do you do? How do you approach it? What should you say?

Make a phone call. Tell the receptionist who answers the phone your name. Explain that you're interested in a modeling career and give her other pertinent information, such as how many and what type of photos you have, whether you have any previous experience, and which area of modeling you're interested in pursuing. If you haven't yet had any photos taken, ask for a list of photographers at this time; it will show that you've done your homework. After the agency employee has information from you, she will most likely give one of the following three responses:

1. **"Send a photo and resume."** Many agencies won't see models under any circumstances until the agency has received a photo and a brief note containing the model's stats and information about his experience. Then, if they think the model shows promise, they will arrange to see him for an interview. Either way, once a model has submitted a photo to an agency for consideration, he should not expect to get it back, even if he encloses a self-addressed, stamped envelope. The photo usually will remain in the agency's file. For this reason, some models submit photocopies of the original prints to save money.

If you've submitted a photo to an agency and you haven't received a response within about two weeks, call the agency and inquire about the status of your photo. "Sometimes we get so overwhelmed with pictures we just file them and don't look at them until the person calls us back," said an agent. "Then when we pull the photo we decide if we want to interview the person. If not, that's when we say, 'Thank you for allowing us to see your photo, you can come and pick it up now if you wish.' "

2. "Come to an open audition." Some agencies hold open auditions or group interviews every two weeks or so. Anyone with an appointment is welcome to attend one of these interviews. During the meeting the agent tells the group about the agency's history and policies, and talks generally about the field of modeling. Then he or she looks at each applicant's photos and briefly speaks to each one individually. When you're invited to attend an open audition, don't accept unless you're certain that you will be able to attend. The word *open* can be deceptive; you may assume the audition will involve a large group of people and that if you don't show up you won't be missed, but this is not the case. Interviews are often limited to ten or fewer attendees. And remember that talent agents aren't just looking for pretty faces; they're looking for responsible, dependable people who are going to act as representatives for their business. If you don't show up or you arrive late, you'll leave a poor first impression. Even though anyone is welcome to an open audition, treat it very seriously.

3. "Come in for a private interview." If you sound very confident and promising over the phone, you may be asked to come in for a private interview. This will involve the same exchanging of information as the open audition, but the agent will spend more time with you one-on-one.

What to Wear Let's say you've made it past the phone call. You've sent photos and a resume, and now you've gotten yourself an interview. What should you wear? "What you wear isn't terribly important as long as you show that you can package yourself nicely. Either wear something neat and professional that you would wear to any other job interview, or dress as you would for your most marketable look: a grandmother type might wear a house dress, a fashion model might wear something stylish, a college type could dress a little preppy. If you come in your look, we'll know you've done your research," said an agent.

What to Bring You should bring all your photos, contact sheets, resumes, and other promotional materials to the interview. Don't worry about impressing the agent with a two hundred dollar portfolio case or millions of photos. "I'm more impressed by people who bring a list of informed questions than by those who sink a lot of money into accessories," said Julie, a pragmatic agent. "I don't expect a huge, elaborate portfolio if you're just starting out in the business."

How to Act "Easygoing confidence impresses me more than any other single quality," explained an agent. "I realize it's natural to be a bit nervous. But if a woman is falling apart from nerves just from meeting little ol' me, what's she going to behave like on a cattle call or a real job?

"Just be yourself. I want to know who *you* are, not who you think you should be. If a person seems too needy, nervous, chatty, or demanding of attention, I'm very hesitant to work with them," said Julie, an agent.

Multiple Listings In cities like New York and Los Angeles, a model can only be represented by one agency at a time. This is called "being exclusive." There are some cities, however, where a model can be listed with every agency in town if she so desires. This is called "multiple listing."

Multiple listing seems to be firmly entrenched in some places, but it causes headaches for models and agents alike. "The agent simply becomes an answering service. She doesn't promote her people as much as she would if they were exclusive because she doesn't want to work her fingers to the bone for a model if a client may turn around and book the model through another agent. So instead of getting out there and humping it, the agent sits back and lets the model do her own promotion, and then the agent waits for the phone to ring."

Even in towns where multiple listings are the norm, each agency has between twenty and two hundred exclusively listed models, usually their top talent. This may seem like a perfect solution to the multiple listing problem—just have everyone go exclusive with one agency! But it's not that simple.

Every agent I interviewed recommended that a model *not* go exclusive under any circumstances during her first year in the business. They advised models to work with several agents first to find out who they feel most comfortable with and who gets them the most bookings.

But while every agency warned strongly against going exclusive with their competition, they all claimed to treat their own exclusive talent like royalty. They said things like "I make sure all my exclusives get first crack at all the jobs because I know I'm their only hope; they can't just turn around and get booked by someone else."

TWENTY

ONCE YOU'RE LISTED

You've done it! You found an agency; you had a successful interview; and the agent asked you to list with her. Congratulations, you have an agent. But what happens now?

CONTRACT AGREEMENTS

You won't be asked to sign a contract unless you're going exclusive. If you are signing an exclusive contract, the duration of the agreement can vary from one, two, and even five years. Find out what your options are. Some agencies only have one standard contract, and some are willing to negotiate certain points. Many exclusive contracts can be broken by the model if she gives sufficient notice—usually sixty days. Some contracts are automatically renewed at the end of their duration unless the model gives notice in advance that he wishes to terminate the contract; if you sign one of these contracts, be aware of the beginning and ending dates, or you could wind up doing a double stint against your will. As in any business transaction, don't sign anything until you've read it carefully. If there are points of the contract you don't understand, don't be afraid to ask questions; you won't seem stupid.

If you're joining an agency in a multiple listing town and you're not going exclusive, you'll probably just be asked to fill out an information card with your name, age, address, stats, and special skills. Your snapshot, comp, or Xerox copy of your photo will be stapled to the information card.

Procedures "Once we've got them signed up, we take care of the pictures first thing. We can't send them out to see clients unless they've got a few good shots to show them. So if the model doesn't have enough pictures, we try to arrange some tests for her or send her to a good

photographer or two to start her portfolio. And if she has any rough spots—say she needs work on makeup application—we send her to one of our models who tutors. Then we send her on some auditions, possibly give her a limited list of clients to call on or send comps to, and possibly send out some mailings about her to let people know we've got a new face," said Diane, owner of New Faces Agency.

Diane continued, "We don't just hand the poor thing a client list with hundreds of names on it and tell her to go out and sell herself. It's frustrating for the model, and it's aggravating for the clients. They don't have the time to visit with every model in town regardless of whether they even need her type. So we send our people out to see just a handful of clients whom we think might have a need for her. It takes the stress off everyone."

At the Eleanor Moore Agency, the procedure for new models goes like this: "We get a comp put together if possible, and send the model out to see a few clients. She'll probably have at least a couple of go-sees in the first week that she's with us; but realistically, it will take her at least a couple of months to really get rolling."

"We send out a few shots of her to clients to test the water and see what their reaction is," said Mary, booker at Susan Wehmann Agency. "Usually they're thrilled to see new talent. If the response is good, we send the model on a go-see or two. If she's prompt, makes a good impression, and is easy to work with, we start to promote her full-force."

Your Responsibilities Once you're registered, you have certain responsibilities to your agent. You should have an answering machine or service, a beeper, or at the very least, a family member or roommate who faithfully takes down your messages and forwards them to you. You must make yourself available as much as possible for auditions and cattle calls, not just jobs. You must keep your agent posted as to your availability; if you'll be out of town or otherwise indisposed, be sure to let her know. If you change your job, address, or phone number, it only takes a second to call your agent and let her know, and it saves her the time and embarrassment of calling your old number and hearing 'Sorry, there's no one here by that name.' "

Your Promotional Options You have the right to be informed of your promotional options. Many agencies use one or more of the following methods to expose the clients to their talent, both old and new:

1. The Headsheet. Most agencies have what is called a *headsheet* or *headbook*, which is printed every year. It might be a poster, a bound or unbound book, a pamphlet, or even a calendar. The headsheet includes a head shot of each model and his or her stats and specialties. Usually, a model must pay a fee to be included in the headsheet. The fee covers printing and mailing costs.

2. The Composite Book. Many agencies have a bound or loose book of composite photos of all their talent. If the book is bound, it's important to submit your composite to the agent before the printing deadline, since loose comps submitted to the client late are often misplaced or discarded. If, on the other hand, the book is loose (for this type, holes are usually punched out of the comps for inclusion in a three-ring notebook), your comp will probably be added to the book no matter when the client receives it. For composite books, the comps are printed en masse through the agency in the same format, which saves the models money.

3. Mailings. Some agents promote their new talent to clients with a monthly or bi-monthly newsletter or other type of mailed message that introduces new individuals. The costs of reproducing photos and printing are usually passed on to the model.

4. Client Lists. Some agencies offer the new model a list of clients to call on, meet in person, and show their portfolios. Other agencies frown on this practice and prefer to send their models to clients more selectively or to simply wait for auditions or cattle calls for the two to meet.

Billing Rate You have the right to know the rate at which your agent is billing out your services. While it's very uncommon, I have heard of one instance where an agency told their models they were being billed out at fifty dollars

per hour, when they were actually being billed out at seventy dollars per hour, and the agency was keeping the difference. If your agent refuses to tell you what your billing rate is, or if she tells you a rate that is lower than the average for your town, you could have reason to be suspicious.

Agent Percentage You also have the right to know what percentage the agency retains from your pay. Most keep 15 percent.

Agent Contact You have the right to expect a certain amount of communication and contact with your agent, but you don't want her to feel as though you're pressuring her, whining, or trying to demand work she doesn't have for you. If you haven't heard from your agent in two or three weeks, it's OK to give her a call and say, "Hi, this is Jane Doe. I was just wondering if you had anything for me this week," or to tell her about any new shots you've had taken, any modeling jobs you've had, or related classes you're taking. This will remind her that you're available and interested in working. Don't call too frequently or demand to know why you aren't being sent out more. If you're unsure about how often your agent is comfortable hearing from you, ask her; she will give you an honest answer.

PROTOCOL
There are certain unspoken rules of protocol that are worth your while to learn when you deal with agents.

1. In multiple listing towns, it's known and accepted by models and agents alike that most talent are represented by several agencies. However, no agent wants to have that fact waved in her face. So if one of your agents gets you a booking, don't call the other one and say, "ABC Company got me this job. Why aren't you sending me out more?" You should, however, be sure to tell all of your agents when you've had a job or to send them a tear sheet, so they're aware of any experience you get that makes you a more marketable and valuable model.

2. Never try to play one agent against another. For instance, if you say, "ABC Company bills me out at ninety-dollars per hour. Why do you bill me out at sixty-five?" You may wind up with no agent at all.

3. Never crash an audition by claiming you were sent by your agent if you weren't. Even if it's a cattle call involving 150 models, you still could be found out, and it will get back to your agent, especially if you were chosen.

4. If you find out about a go-see your agent didn't send you on, don't call her to ask why you weren't included, even if you think you were perfect for it. If she thought you were right for it, she would have sent you. Don't annoy her by questioning her judgment.

TWENTY-ONE

LIVE RUNWAY MODELS

Even after you've listed with an agency, there are still some areas of modeling you will need to explore on your own as a freelancer. Three of these areas are formal live runway modeling, informal live runway modeling, and modeling for hair salons. I will cover them in chapters twenty-one through twenty-three.

The main reason most agencies don't represent their talent in these areas is simply because the pay tends to be considerably lower than it is for print or broadcast modeling, so it's simply not worth their time involvement.

When you are working as a freelancer promoting yourself for live runway modeling, you will have to try harder to break in, to find out where the jobs are, and to get yourself interviews with runway coordinators. It takes more effort than just sitting by the phone and waiting for your agent to call you with an audition. It's harder work than print modeling, the time commitment is greater, and sometimes the fittings, rehearsals, and the show itself are held in different places. As I mentioned, the pay is lower than for other types of modeling and the rewards are less tangible since you don't have pictures or anything to show for your effort when the show is over, yet most of the models I interviewed who had experienced both print and live modeling said they enjoyed runway the best of all. Why?

It's more of a challenge; it feels more glamorous; you have total contact with your audience and immediate response to your work; and at times the atmosphere backstage can be very exciting, almost electric.

WHO CAN BE A LIVE RUNWAY MODEL?
Who are the runway coordinators looking for? What look?

What height, weight, and size? What age? What special talents?

The Look The restrictions on how a runway model should look are far fewer than on the appearance of print models. Runway models can have the MOR look, as do most catalog models, but they can also look much more exotic, more ethnic, even more severe. Whereas most successful print models have very regular features, runway models often have one or more outstanding features—an unusual nose, an extremely broad face, markedly full lips.

Height, Weight, and Size The height, weight, and size requirements for runway are much the same as those for print fashion: 5'7" to 5'11", weight proportionate to height, clothing sizes 6, 8, and a few 10s, shoe size is variable.

Age I have met runway models who are working successfully at ages eighteen to fifty. Mature women are being used more and more for runway, since they are often the buying market to which these shows are aimed.

Walk A runway model should have a natural, graceful way of walking with long strides. She should be able to walk comfortably even in very high heels and be able to execute half and full turns both to the right and to the left. These turns aren't complicated to learn, but they're difficult to describe in print. To learn them, go to a fashion show or two and watch the pros in action; then practice at home. Or call an agency for the name of a runway model who is willing to tutor.

Remember that walking doesn't just involve your legs; it involves your whole body—your torso, your arms—and a good posture and attitude. Dance classes and athletic experience can help.

Posing For some shows, models are required to strike a pose and freeze onstage while other models walk the runway. Sometimes the pose implies a natural stance; sometimes the pose is more editorial and requires the model's creativity. Many experienced runway models have two or three stock poses for different clothing styles that they use in a pinch so they're never caught off balance at a rehearsal. Practice some poses of your own at home.

Personal Style Every runway model has her own personal style. One woman I know is naturally friendly and exuberant even when she's not on stage. So when she does a show, she plays up her real personality, walking with a springy step, waving to the audience, smiling, and making lots of eye contact. Another model, equally in demand, is naturally quite shy and reserved, so she uses this aspect of her personality when she's modeling to come across as mysterious and sultry. Take an honest look at your real personality; then use it for your live modeling.

HOW TO FIND THE WORK
If your agent won't represent you, how can you find live modeling work?

● Ask your agent for a list of department store and independent live runway coordinators.

● Talk to other models to find out who the coordinators are and how to get in touch with them.

● Anytime you see a fashion show being advertised, call the establishment sponsoring it and ask for the name and number of the coordinator.

● Keep an eye on country clubs, nightclubs, hair salons, exclusive clothing boutiques, and design schools and colleges that have good fashion design programs. These often put on shows and may be good places for a novice to start.

Auditioning What should you wear to an audition for live runway modeling, and what might you be asked to do? You should always wear at least a moderately high heel to show that you can indeed walk comfortably in them. An outfit that is stylish and shows your body lines is preferable, along with soft, natural makeup and hair.

The coordinator will want to see any photos and comps you have and will ask about related experience. She will probably ask you to walk for her and to execute full and half turns. She also might ask you to walk in several different manners—pretending you're wearing an elegant evening gown, then pretending you're wearing a tennis outfit, for instance—so she can see how well you project different moods.

Just as when you went to your agent interview, it's important that you appear as relaxed and comfortable as possible.

YOUR FIRST SHOW
If your audition is successful and the coordinator books you for a show, your first task will be to go to your fitting. Always wear or bring nude hose; a backless, strapless bra; and dress shields to a fitting. The next step will be the rehearsal. It will probably take place on the same stage where the actual show will be. You'll probably receive a sheet of instructions telling you in what order you'll appear onstage and what you'll wear during each appearance. Then the coordinator will line up the models (remember which models are in front and behind you) and ask them to do a walk-through, literally walk through the show, to get a feel for the timing of exits and entrances. If they need you to execute special moves, there will be a choreographer at the rehearsal to teach them to you.

Some rehearsals are quick and easy, lasting only an hour or two. Others that involve more complicated staging may last an entire day, and I've even heard of them running into the night if things don't go smoothly.

Some runway coordinators don't mind if you bring a friend along to sit quietly and watch the rehearsal; others don't allow this. If you're not sure of your coordinator's preference, don't risk alienating her by bringing an extra person.

For the actual show, you will be assigned a dresser, a person who helps you get in and out of your wardrobe and organizes the clothing and accessories for you. Timing is critical. Sometimes the amount of time you have to change seems impossibly short. Often, you won't be able to make it back to the dressing room; your dresser will meet you just offstage with your change of wardrobe, and you'll have to disrobe without any privacy. So if you're painfully modest, this is not the area of modeling for you!

During a show, everyone is in a hurry. You not only must be responsible for getting your own changes and entrances correct, you have to make sure you're not in anyone else's way, as well. And after dashing backstage to make your hectic changes, you have to be able to appear onstage again, unruffled and picture perfect.

"It can get pretty wild," said Joel, a male runway model. "One time I was in a show and a model who was supposed to be in the final segment couldn't make the change in time. I was his size, so I had to jump into his suit and do the segment for him, with no warning, no rehearsal, and of course I hadn't been shown the moves. But I survived."

A classically Nordic-looking male model said, "Yes, there are some funny things that happen at live shows. Once I did a live show in a shopping mall, not realizing that there was a space in the facade that the audience could see through to the backstage area where I was changing for each segment.

"Another time I was in a style show that featured rainwear for women. I was supposed to follow these women out onto the stage and express desire for them as they peeled off their raincoats and laid them on the stage. There had been no rehearsal, so I did the first thing that came to my mind. I very gracefully and sensually bent to the floor and picked up a raincoat in my teeth. The crowd appreciated it."

A female model said, "Undressing in front of other people backstage isn't really that bad because nobody's paying any attention to you—they're all in as big a hurry as you are. The atmosphere is very professional. I never feel like anyone's peeking."

Like any other form of freelancing, you should estab-lish the rate of pay and payment schedule in advance. This will help prevent misunderstandings. Almost all agreements regarding live runway modeling are estab-lished verbally between the runway coordinator and the model. This seems to be protection enough for both parties. One Minneapolis model even won a conciliation court case against a runway coordinator, based solely on the strength of the original verbal agreement between the two.

However, if you feel the need to have a written agreement, the runway coordinator might not object. Said Sue E. Horstman, a successful freelance coordina-tor, "If a model presented me with a letter of agree-ment, I'd be happy to sign it, even though I do all my business verbally. A written agreement would protect me as well as the model, by discouraging models from dropping out of shows after they've been booked."

The pace is hectic, and the emphasis is *not* on the model's comfort during a show. But the glamour is cer-tainly apparent. And the challenge. If you fit the criteria and you think live modeling sounds exciting, give it a try. You'll have a memory to cherish forever.

TWENTY-TWO

INFORMAL LIVE MODELING

There are many opportunities for live, informal modeling in places you might not expect: mall and department store events, boutiques, bridal shops, furriers, nightclubs, country clubs, merchandise markets, business and industry conventions, and the list goes on. While this type of modeling tends not to pay very well, it can be easier to break into, due to less rigid appearance and experience requirements. It's a training ground for beginners that can provide exposure and contacts that could lead to other jobs.

FINDING WORK

Sometimes it isn't easy to find out when this type of work is available. The coordinators don't have budgets big enough to allow them to work through agencies or to advertise for models, so they rely on word of mouth. Small boutiques may approach their favorite, most attractive customers and ask them to model in return for clothing from the store. Since informal modeling is just that, informal, there are no set rules for how the models are retained or for how they're paid. Each situation is different.

Here are some businesses where you might find informal modeling and some advice on how to break into working for them:

Bridal Shops Frequently bridal shops advertise to hire "model/receptionists," meaning that the employee will work primarily as a receptionist and will occasionally be asked to model gowns for individual customers. The pay is usually not much more than for a regular receptionist's job, but unlike other types of modeling, it's steady work. For this type of work, you should have a pleasant voice and manner over the phone and in person, wear an average

clothing size, be exceptionally well-groomed, be able to put customers at ease, and be able to learn the details about merchandise the establishment sells and services it offers.

Boutiques Many small boutiques have informal fashion shows in the spring and fall to draw more customers and kick off their new lines. The shows usually occur in the evening. The models walk through the crowd and chat about the clothing they're presenting. Snacks and beverages are sometimes served.

The models are often regular customers and friends of the proprietors. The best way to get into a show of this type is to simply put out the word; tell everyone you're interested in getting modeling experience. Chances are someone will know someone who knows about an opportunity.

Models are usually paid with clothing items, a discount on clothing purchases, or a gift certificate.

Furriers Furriers often hold informal, or *trunk,* shows in which the models walk through the store telling the customers about the coats they are wearing. Sometimes the models are hired to fill a double position such as sales person or receptionist, just as at the bridal shops. In this area it's very important to develop a relaxed relationship with the customers and to educate yourself about the merchandise.

Shopping Malls Merchants in small shopping malls sometimes present style shows together. The models may be students of nearby modeling schools; sometimes they are customers of the mall merchants; and occasionally they are mall employees themselves. Usually the models are paid with discounts on merchandise and services or with gift certificates.

Department Stores In addition to the enormous, choreographed style shows that turn into media events in some towns, large department stores put on smaller trunk shows in which the models roam through various departments and restaurants during the noon hour, presenting the clothing. These shows can pay better than other forms of informal modeling, but not as well as formal stage shows.

Nightclubs Nightclubs often collaborate with area businesses to put on style shows. These shows are generally quite informal, require no rehearsal, and pay twenty dollars to thirty dollars per show. Some clubs present shows weekly or monthly, and this can give you repeat business if you're talented and cooperative.

Country Clubs Country club fashion shows are organized by freelance coordinators. Make a list of clubs in your area and call for the names and numbers of fashion show coordinators.

Remember that for all types of informal modeling, you should always have with you dress shields and two or three pairs of pantyhose. You must be careful not to get makeup on the clothing, and never smoke, eat, or paint your nails once you are dressed for the show. The clothing will go back to the racks for sale after you're finished, so they have to be in brand new condition.

CREATE YOUR OWN DEMAND

Perhaps you've put out your feelers and done your investigating, but you still haven't found any informal, live modeling opportunities. What then? Well, you can create your own demand by becoming your own freelance coordinator. It's a real challenge, but it's not as difficult as it sounds.

1. Gather five to ten models (including several men) who, like yourself, are interested in getting live modeling experience and are willing to work in exchange for merchandise or discounts on goods and services.

2. Approach several small businesses that are in the same mall or near each other: one or two clothing stores, a hair salon, and a shop that sells jewelry or accessories would be a good start. Offer to coordinate a style show for them in their mall or, if there is no common enclosure, arrange to have the show at a nearby nightclub or restaurant. You should be prepared to act as liaison between the businesses to determine a location, date, and time. You will also be responsible for the requisition and safe return of the clothing each model will wear. Check with established coordinators to see what they charge for their services in your area. Charge accordingly, or start with a slightly lower fee.

3. Ask the merchants how much, if any, money is available to promote the show. Promotion could be as simple as posting signs in the mall or nightclub, or it could involve more extensive efforts. For instance, many stores have mailing lists of preferred clients. If you design a flyer announcing the show, perhaps each business would be willing to absorb the expense of sending out a mailing to the customers on their lists.

Coordinating fashion shows requires some organizational skills. You'll need to divide the whole project into individual steps (sort of bite-sized pieces). For your first show, leave yourself more time than you think you'll need to work out the particulars and pull the whole thing together. Then, after you've gained some experience, you can give yourself shorter deadlines.

The best times to approach businesses and propose shows like this are spring and fall, since these are the seasons when new fashions and hairstyles appear.

If you have a little ambition, you may find that you enjoy coordinating style shows as much as you enjoy the modeling that got you involved in the shows in the first place.

TWENTY-THREE

*H*AIR SALON SHOWS

Many hair salons recruit both amateur and professional models for style shows they give regularly, sometimes for several shows a year. The shows may involve walking a runway; sometimes the stylist actually styles, cuts, or chemically processes the hair onstage while the audience watches. Some shops hang huge posters of their own stylist's work in their shops, and some hairdressers need models for photos of their work to submit to publications. Occasionally shops need models for local advertisements.

Generally, modeling for a hair salon only pays with the services rendered for the show or shots, plus hair care products, photos, T-shirts, or other items. But of course the model also gains experience and exposure.

It's relatively easy to break into modeling for hair salons, and many successful models have started their careers this way. Salons that need models advertise in the classified section of the newspaper, notify agencies, and post signs in their shop windows and on notice boards.

Although modeling for a hair salon might be a good starting point for you, just remember that whatever is done to your hair for the live show or photos should not be so exotic that it would interfere with your other modeling. For instance, if you're a young mom type, you shouldn't allow a stylist to give you an outrageous, new wave hairstyle. And any coloring or permanent wave added to your hair should look soft and natural. "I let a stylist color my hair plum-violet because I thought that even though I usually got auditions for conservative-looking business types, most of the work was shot in black and white and since the added color was the same tone as my natural color, I figured it would be OK. It wasn't. I walked into auditions and the casting person would look at me like, 'Who sent us this creature with the purple hair?' Even though it photographed the same in black and white, it gave them the wrong impression of me and turned them off. The color lasted almost three months, and I didn't work once during that time," said a model who learned her lesson the hard way.

Also consider that if you've already invested money in professional photos, any dramatic change in your hairstyle will render them useless. You'll have to pay for new shots. So it's very important to establish at the initial consultation what you will and will not allow to be done to your hair. You can't afford to be wishy-washy. If you're too meek about stating the limits, the stylist may just go ahead and do whatever he or she wants to do to you, anyway. One good way to help yourself avoid trouble is to take a good look at the shop and its stylists. Does the shop have leopard-spotted wallpaper and a fuchsia floor? Does the hair of the stylists match that decor? If so, you may be better off to forget about modeling for them and to find a nice, quiet, MOR shop to launch your career for you instead.

Sometimes it's hard to know what to veto and what to accept in style, chemical processing, and cut. This is especially true if you haven't experimented much with your hair on your own and you don't know how it behaves when given certain treatments. Below is a list to help you determine what procedures are safe for you to indulge in, and what to avoid.

HAIR STYLES AND CUTS

As I mentioned earlier, a dramatic hairstyle change can cost you a lot in new pictures, composites, and time. If you're getting modeling work with the hairstyle you al-

These are samples of shots taken for hair salons.

While most hair salon shots do not have the earmarks of the typical "introductory head shot," they are still excellent additions to any model's port-folio.

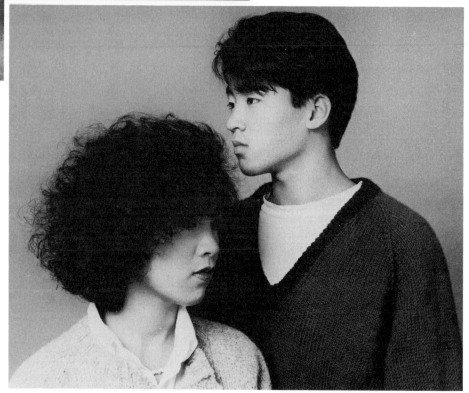

ready have, be cautious when considering a change. Only accept a totally new hairstyle if it meets the following criteria:

1. You've determined in advance what changes you would find acceptable and you won't allow yourself to be talked into something you haven't had time to think about.

2. You've bounced the idea of the new style off of your agent and friends, and they seem receptive.

3. You've worked with the stylist and used every ounce of communication skills you've got to agree on a style that meets both your expectations and his, so that neither of you will be surprised or disappointed by the outcome.

Permanents A good perm can add body and manageability to your hair, but a bad perm can make you look like Little Orphan Annie or worse. Perming previously chemically-treated or otherwise damaged hair can have devastating results. So if the stylist wants to give you a perm, only consider it if your hair is in excellent condition and it hasn't had a lot of other processing. The new salon perms are very gentle and are often used only at the base of the hairs (near the scalp) to give lift, rather than curl.

There are many different types of perms, which vary in harshness. Find out what all your options are and stress to the stylist that you want a soft, natural look. Also remember that perms that add curl can make the hair appear shorter, so make sure that your hair is long enough to compensate for this.

Temporary Color Temporary color can add body, shine, and depth to hair. However, too many applications can coat the hair shafts, weigh them down, and cause dullness and damage. If the temporary color is applied to damaged or porous hair, the color can "take" in an uneven, dark, and unnatural way. And different hair types behave differently when they're colored. Fine, healthy hair has flat hair shafts and doesn't take the color deposits easily. Coarse or curly hair has more wavy shafts and may take the color more readily. If you do opt for a temporary color treatment, ask for one that has little or no peroxide; this will ensure that the hair will be its natural color when the coloring washes out. Temporary coloring that requires a large amount of peroxide can leave the hair bleached out and dull when it wears off. Red color bases tend to cling the longest; colors with an ashy or neutral base are less tenacious. Occasionally a color that is meant to wash out in six to eight weeks permanently alters the color of the hair. This is a risk you must consider with chemical process; the results are not totally predictable.

Permanent Color Permanent color treatments involve peroxide, which lifts away some of the natural color of the hair. When the color softens or bleeds out, you are sometimes left with a lighter color than you started with. The term *permanent color* is somewhat misleading, since no color treatment is entirely permanent; they all mellow or wash away with time. Sun, wind, blow dryers, and products containing alcohol all speed up the color loss.

As with perms, the hair should be in excellent condition for predictable, even, long-lasting color results. As with temporary color, too many applications one on top of the next can be damaging.

Permanent coloring should be applied in a tone and color similar to your natural color so there's a less noticeable difference as the hair is growing out. If the color you choose is very different, you may need frequent retouching at the roots.

Since peroxide ruffles the hair shafts and can be drying, you need to take extra care when maintaining color-treated hair. Use shampoo that is especially formulated for chemically-processed hair; go easy on the blow-drying; and cover your head in the sun and wind.

Permanent colors that are applied to only part of the hair, with techniques like foiling or painting, give body and richness with less damage to the hair, and the color looks more natural when the hair is growing out.

Bleaching Women and men with dark blonde or light brown hair can add depth and highlights by lightening small sections of hair, such as with foiling or painting techniques. This type of highlighting can give the impression of overall blondeness without the risk of bleaching all of your hair.

Overall bleaching can be a risky proposition. The effect is achieved in two steps: first, the natural color is lightened, or *stripped;* then the hair is *toned*—ash, red, or neutral tones are added. The bleach is damaging to the hair; and the results are less natural-looking than highlighting because all the hairs turn the same shade and color so there is little depth. Also, the results can be unpredictable. The more shades you lighten, the riskier the procedure.

Those interested in modeling careers should never make drastic color changes, especially not into the stark platinum blonde shades. Hair those shades photographs poorly; it loses detail and provides little contrast with skin tones in b&w. A soft, highlighted blonde is better.

If you follow the advice outlined in this chapter, you will be able to gain experience as a hair model without sacrificing your other modeling opportunities.

TWENTY-FOUR

SPECIALTY MODELING

Maybe you're still not sure you want to be a model. Perhaps you think you're simply too shy to show your face in front of a camera or an audience. Well, how about showing your hands, legs, or feet? That's right, you can be a specialty model—if you've got gorgeous gams or fabulous fingers.

Of course, if you can do both specialty modeling and fashion or character modeling (or all three) you'll simply have that many more avenues open to you. Sound good? Read on to find out how to break into specialty modeling, and what the requirements are.

BREAKING IN

You break into specialty modeling the same way you break into any other area of modeling: by getting photos and approaching an agency. The same photographers who shoot head and body shots also shoot hands, legs, and feet, as well as other specialties. Just as for fashion and character shooting, the best way to find a photographer is to call an agency and ask for a list. Then go through all the comparative shopping steps recommended in chapter fourteen.

When you find a photographer you want to work with, set an appointment and discuss the best way to present your specialty. Should you use props? If so, what sort? What props does the photographer have available for you? What props do you have at home? Where can you rent props? How many setups is the photographer willing to do per roll? With specialty shots, there are fewer variables than with shots involving the whole body or the face, so he may be willing to do more looks per roll for you. When I shoot hands, I can usually get enough good shots in different scenarios for the model to put together a whole composite from just two rolls.

Once you've got your contact sheet from the photographer, follow the same procedure as you would for selecting fashion and character shots. See chapter sixteen.

Requirements

Hands   Many people are under the mistaken impression that to be a successful hand model, all you need are long nails. This simply isn't the case. In face, there is little call for hands with glamour-length fingernails. Aspiring hand models only need neatly manicured nails of uniform length. In the rare instances where longer nails are required, there are many artificial types available. The important requirements involve the hands themselves.

To assess your hands and determine if you have what it takes for hand modeling, hold your arms above your head and wiggle your fingers for one or two minutes; this allows the veins in your hands to constrict. Then lower your hands and, with the fingers pointing up, look at your palms and at the backs. Do you have any unusual or pronounced folds in your palms, or are they unobtrusive and pleasant-looking? Do you have large knuckles and pronounced wrinkles on the knuckle area, or are they smooth and proportionate with the rest of each finger? Do you have any scars on your hands? Any pronounced veins? Broken blood vessels? Age spots? Freckles?

If your hands are smooth and free of any of the blemishes I've just listed, you're probably a good candidate for hand modeling. Don't worry if your fingers aren't unusually long; women with small hands and average length fingers can get work that requires moms' hands.

These first two shots were from a collage an art director created for a fashion mailer. Each photo highlights different accessories and body parts. For the first one, we could have used a fashion model with good hands, or a hand model with a small waist. We chose the former.

This shot required a male fashion model with a great jaw and good lip definition.

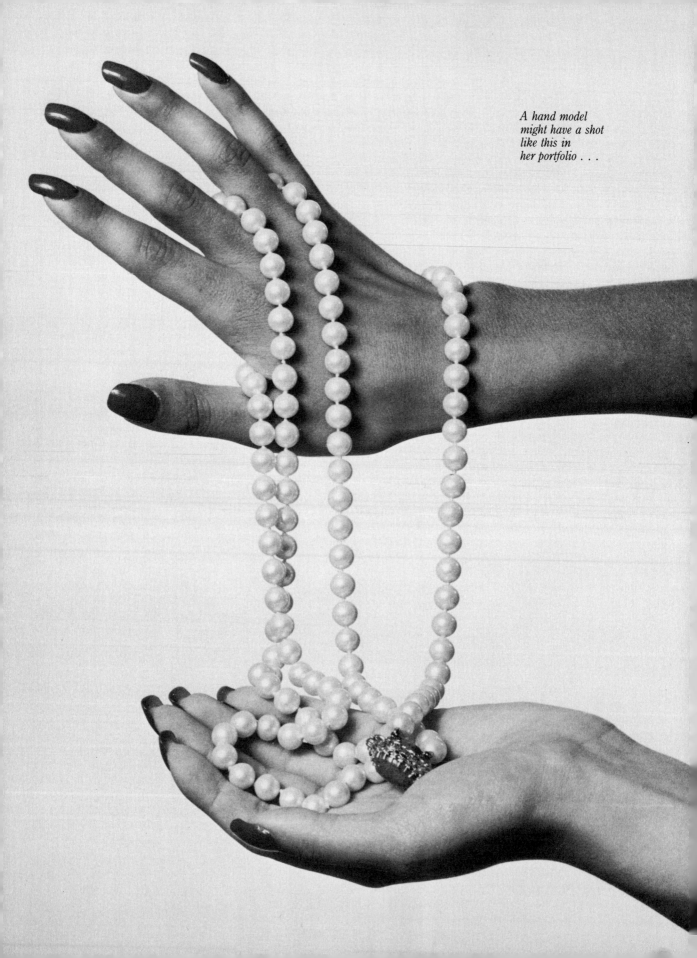

A hand model might have a shot like this in her portfolio . . .

. . . and a leg model
might have a
shot like this.

Men with well cared for, smaller sized hands are often hired when the client wants its product to appear larger than it really is. Men with large, rugged hands can get work for farmers' and workmen's hands.

When you plan your photos to kick off your hand modeling career, keep your market in mind. Are there a lot of medical supply companies in your area? Then do a shot with beakers or microscope slides or a stethoscope. Contrast it with a shot that shows your hand type. For a young mom's hands, try a product shot with dish soap or perhaps a shot of your hands applying a Band-Aid adhesive strip to a child's knee. If you have long, gorgeous fingers, try a shot using jewelry or cosmetics as props. Some models like to use props that are a little unexpected, such as a flute with a flower coming out of its end, or a goldfish in a brandy snifter, because they think it helps to draw the client's attention. Men should have shots of their hands holding tools, a remote control for television, a fishing rod, or other such props. At least one of your shots should show part of your palm, to indicate that it has no flaws.

Hand models need to practice extra special skin care for their hands. Some models sleep with their hands in lotion-filled gloves every night. Others are more casual about their hand care. You'll have to find a routine that works for you.

Legs and Feet In the world of modeling, legs and feet usually go hand in hand. (Pardon the pun.) Leg models must also be good foot models, and to be a good foot model you generally have to be able to fit into a size 6½ sample shoe. There are many tall fashion models with beautiful, shapely, long legs, but they inevitably require a larger shoe size. Can you imagine a 5′10″ woman being able to balance on tiny size 6½ feet? This opens up the leg and foot market to more petite women, as long as their legs are proportioned nicely.

Leg and foot models are sometimes called upon to model sandals, which expose parts of the bare foot. So, if you've got beautiful feet, include a shot of them in your portfolio or composite. (Remember that skin care and pedicures are important for feet that will be photographed.) For best results elevate your feet for a minute or two before shooting (as you would your hands).

Leg and foot shots are greatly enhanced by the right props, just as hand shots are. A photo showing beautiful, bare legs and feet could include an atomizer, a bottle of lotion, an attractively draped towel or a robe. For shots showing legs and feet that are wearing shoes, locations add interest.

Remember that the camera picks up every little detail, so all hose, shoes, and accessories used in this type of shot must be immaculate.

Other Specialties A demand for other specialties some-times arises, but it's difficult to build a whole career around them, since the demand is so sporadic. For instance, models are sometimes hired for their lips, lips and teeth, hair, tummies, eyes, and noses. Since there are very few models who specialize exclusively in any of these areas, generally fashion models who have one or more of these outstanding characteristics are usually cast for these jobs. Since work that requires isolated body parts or facial features is so rare, you needn't rush out to get this type of photo for your portfolio. But if you have noteworthy lips and teeth, or any other feature, you may eventually want to add a shot of it to your portfolio so your agent will think of you if the need for it arises. If you don't want to go to the expense of shooting a photo for such an unusual area of work, at least verbally bring your special feature or features to the attention of your agent and include it in the stats on your comp.

Specialty modeling can be just as lucrative and rewarding as other types of modeling. The only drawback is that when your hands or feet appear in a TV commercial or a print ad, your friends might not recognize them as yours. "I was with a friend watching TV one night when a commercial with my hands in it came on. I said, 'That's me,' and she said, 'Yeah, sure.' People don't believe me, or they just don't get as excited about it as they would if it were my face they saw in an ad," said Mardi, a hand model. "But I make money at it; that's the important part to me."

Specialty modeling can also greatly enhance your endeavors in other modeling areas. "I do fashion and hand modeling. Frequently I'll go in for a hand shoot and the client or the photographer will say, 'Gee, you've got a great face, too.' And, wouldn't you know it, two or three weeks down the road, I'll get a call from the same people asking me to do fashion or young mom. It just helps me make all sorts of contacts," said a happy model.

So whether your primary interest is fashion modeling or you simply want to stick to your one or two special features, specialty modeling can help you build your earning potential and visibility. If you've got the characteristics and qualities it takes, why not give it a try?

TWENTY-FIVE

*B*ROADCAST MODELING

Many models who have been working in print for a while eventually wonder if they can make the leap into broadcast modeling. Some successful broadcast models did, indeed, get their starts as print models. Print modeling experience can help you break into broadcast in several ways. Broadcast bookers and print bookers work in the same offices, often side-by-side. When you go in to see your print agent, your face will become familiar to the broadcast people. And if you've proved yourself to your print agent as dependable, well-prepared, and talented, she may put in a good word for you to her broadcast counterpart or help to arrange a meeting with her for you. And print modeling gives you experience in an audition situation. Therefore, it can help take the edge off your nervousness when you go to a more demanding broadcast situation, where you might be required to read or improvise lines.

MAKE YOURSELF MARKETABLE

But broadcast modeling requires special skills, talents, and presence that print does not, and the competition is fierce. There are steps that you, as a print model, must take in order to make yourself more marketable as a broadcast model before attempting an interview with a broadcast agent.

Acting and Voice Training "Acting experience is a must," said a broadcast agent. "I don't even want to interview people if they haven't taken any acting classes or acted in community or semi-pro theater. And voice training helps, too. Do anything you can to get experience, broaden your acting range, and prove that you're serious, that this is not just a whim of yours, but a real aspiration."

If you have some acting experience and you're ready to approach a broadcast agent, where do you start?

Photo and Resume Just as with print modeling, agents are often unwilling to meet people until they have access to their photos and resumes. A fashion head shot won't work; the resume head shot should look natural and friendly, with little makeup and a simple shirt or sweater that doesn't "type" you. Theatrical shots with black turtlenecks and pensive expressions are no good, either. There is no substitute for a simple, straightforward resume shot.

The resume itself should include your name, vital statistics, education, all acting experience, brief mention of your print modeling experience, and any special talents such as musical instruments, singing, dancing, even skiing, roller skating, and motorcycle riding. You never know what small quirky skill could help to land you a role in a commercial.

The Audition If the agent likes your photo and resume and asks you to come in for an audition, what should you expect? What qualities will he be looking for in you at this meeting?

Most likely he'll ask you to do a cold reading. You may be asked to read a single script as a variety of characters or to read from several different scripts. "I'm looking for a calm, confident reading, with lots of eye contact. If the actor can't make eye contact, he or she won't be a good seller. I watch for good quality and versatility of character interpretation; good voice quality, range, and projection; an expressive face; good body language; and whether or not the person follows direction well. What he or she looks like

isn't very important to me, as long as the person can put himself together well. There's a place for many different looks and types, although there isn't as much in broadcast for older children nor very exotic types. An average, pleasant-looking person or a character has the biggest share of this market," explained a broadcast booker.

To prepare yourself for an interview with a broadcast agent, try doing cold readings for friends and family. Ask them to throw out different characters and emotions for you to portray. Try some improvisation in which you and another person set up a scene, choose some characters, and make up the script as you go along. Anything you can do to make yourself feel relaxed and confident about performing will enhance your chances of having a successful audition.

Once You're Listed If the broadcast agent likes your audition and asks you to list with his department, he'll start to send you out for go-sees. He may send you out for principal roles right away, or he may send you out for nonspeaking roles initially to allow you to become accustomed to the field. Remember, there are no small parts, just small actors. So never turn down any audition or role because you think you're too important or too talented for it; you would be passing up invaluable experience, exposure, and contacts.

If the agent is very enthusiastic about you, he may ask you to put together a voice tape. The tape is usually about three minutes long and includes scripts from three or four spots, each about sixty seconds long, that were taken either from real commercials or were written especially to show off your special characters and talents. Your tape should express your full acting range, so choose pieces that contrast, perhaps something comic, something upbeat, something serious, and something authoritative. Your agent will help you put your tape together. There is some expense involved. An average 3 minute tape can cost anywhere from $200 to $400 to create. Your main cost is recording studio time, which can run as high as $75 per hour, so you can keep your cash outlay to a minimum with extra preparation on your scripts before you enter the studio.

Theater Work Even if you're registered with a broadcast agent and you're getting regular commercial work, it's still helpful to pursue roles in theater productions. "You don't just stop growing as an actor once you get commercial work. Getting listed is not this stagnant thing, like arriving

An example of broadcast, or "resume," photos. Notice the straightforward posing, plain background, high energy, and excellent eye contact.

at the end of a journey. You have to keep honing your skill, developing your acting," said John, a successful broadcast model. Luckily, most theater auditions, rehearsals, and performances take place at night and on weekends, so they don't interfere with commercial work.

BROADCAST VS PRINT WORK

How do models think broadcast work compares with print work?

"Broadcast is harder, no doubt about that," said Barry, a model who's worked in both. "You have to learn lines, and you have to have this intangible thing called 'timing,' you have to project emotion and mood, not just with your face and body, like in print, but with your voice, as well. You have to really 'be there,' in character, every second. You have to do more waiting around and more takes of the same thing over and over, and still be fresh and energetic."

"The pay is great. Residuals are like money out of the sky. But you really earn it, because you have to be someone else with every fiber of your being for that whole shot, which often lasts the entire day. You have to be able to give the director exactly what he wants even when he doesn't know what he wants himself," said David.

"I started out in theater with absolutely no intention of ever pursuing commercial acting—and boy, was I a snob. I thought the theater was art and broadcast acting was prostitution. And I thought broadcast would be so easy. You know, you see the woman on TV scrubbing her toilet and you think, 'How hard can that be?' Finally I tried my hand at broadcast modeling just in an effort to pay the rent. I found out fast that it isn't easy; you have to be a damned good actress to make people believe that you are a real housewife enjoying yourself scrubbing that toilet. It really is an art."

So broadcast modeling is harder, and it does require more training, skill, patience, and timing than print modeling. But the rewards do seem to compensate for the added effort.

Being an Extra There is one role that some aspiring broadcast models snub their noses at, possibly to the detriment of their careers. I'm talking about the role of an extra.

The very word implies something superfluous, something that can easily be done without. Being an extra in a movie, a commercial, an industrial film, or a video seems to be the least glamorous, appreciated, or lauded function that one can perform as "talent." The hours can be excruciatingly long; the pay is low; the work involves a lot of waiting and being herded around; and I've heard complaints that extras are treated less than royally by some directors and production assistants. To top it off,

after long hours at low pay, you may wind up cut out of the project altogether in the editing process or as an unidentifiable speck in the background. So why bother?

"Because it's fun," said a woman who's been an extra in five television commercials. "You get to be in a commercial. You sometimes get to have outfit changes and practice your acting (even when you're just part of the background, you still have to act). You get free lunch, a chance to meet people and make contacts, and a break from the everyday grind. The money may not be great, but it's more than I'd make at my regular job in the same amount of hours." Extras earn an average of one hundred dollars per day.

And there's one very large benefit to being an extra that occurs more often than you might think; sometimes an extra gets bumped up into a principal role.

"I got a principal role for a beer commercial that I never would have been considered for because I had no broadcast experience," said Joel, a model who had only print experience. "I was supposed to be part of the crowd in this bar scene. A guy who was supposed to be a principal was getting fitted before the shoot, and someone suddenly asked him his age. He was nineteen—too young to be in a commercial for an alcoholic beverage legally. So they were in a bind. They were all ready to shoot with no principal, so they asked me to step in. Of course, I happily complied. If I hadn't been an extra, I would never have had a shot at that role."

"I was at my very first commercial job as an extra," said Henry, a fifty-one-year-old character actor, "and they asked me to stand behind the bar and bartend. Then I mugged a little and the director liked it, so he kept asking me to ham it up more and more. He wound up using a close-up of my face to end the commercial. I made some good residuals on that."

"I was at a job that lasted eleven hours," said Monica, a young woman who had no aspirations of becoming a broadcast model, but took the job as a lark. "It really dragged on, and everyone was crabby and trying not to show it. At the very end of the shooting, when all the principals had finished, the director called it a wrap, and we were all relieved. But then he changed his mind and said he wanted the extras to stay for a minute. We groaned. He picked out five of us to solo in front of the camera for close-ups and had each of us improvise some lines. I did a few takes and then went home and didn't

This broadcast head shot shows this actress's special warm quality that casting directors insist on for commercial work. Notice that the wardrobe in this shot is simple, unobtrusive, and doesn't typecast the model in any particular role or character.

think about it, because I knew they had miles of film, and most of it never gets used. But three months later I was watching TV and the ad came on. Near the end there was the close-up of me. It was a real treat. That made the whole thing worthwhile."

Another benefit of acting as an extra is that your casting director or agent will appreciate it, especially if it involves a huge mob scene for which she's having trouble rounding up enough reliable talent. When a juicy role comes up that you might be right for, she's more likely to remember you fondly for stepping in during a pinch, and she might be more likely to give you a crack at it.

And of course, even if you're not featured on camera as an extra, you still get the benefit of being involved in the production, seeing how things work, getting a feel for the atmosphere of the set and the way various directors interact with actors, so you'll be more knowledgeable and calm when you finally get a chance at a big role.

"I learned most of what I know about commercial acting by being an extra. I got to be on the set and watch other actors at work on a real shoot. I got to see how they worked with the director to change and develop their readings and interpretations—how the creative process works. It was a lot more valuable for me than even acting classes. I think anyone who wants to be a commercial actor should work as an extra for several months before they even go to their first audition. Look at it as an apprenticeship," said David, who does broadcast modeling.

"It never hurts to see pros at work," said John, another commercial actor. "You get to observe the dynamics of the relationship between the director and the actors. Then if you ever have an audition for that director—and chances are that in a small market, you will—you'll know if he's laid back and likes lots of input from the talent or if he's more into being the power in the relationship and wants to control the whole shebang. Sometimes just understanding the director's personality and politics can make the difference between success and failure even more than your acting ability."

"It's something you can put on resume, and every little bit helps," said Barbara, an actress. "I was always getting told, 'We like your reading, but you don't have any experience,' so I took anything that came along, no matter how small. It really paid off in experience and contacts. I'm convinced that it helped me land my first principal role in an industrial film. I even did a commercial once that involved over one hundred extras, and I wasn't even on camera; I was 'bleed-off,' but it was a contact."

So if you want to make it as a commercial actor, never turn down any chance to be on a set.

This headshot of Lisa works nicely for a fashion shot, but is too stylized to submit for broadcast modeling jobs. The trendy outfit with layered fabrics is not appropriate for the more "middle of the road" look needed in broadcast work.

CASTING DIRECTORS

If you enter the field of broadcast modeling, sooner or later you will encounter a person called a casting director.

Q. *What is a casting director?*

A. A casting director is someone who is hired by a production company to choose actors and talent to appear in feature and minor films, industrial films, and television commercials and videos.

Q. *How are they different from agents?*

A. An agent doesn't have the power to cast an actor or model in a particular role; she simply sends the actor to an audition. She can give the client feedback about who she thinks would be right for the particular role, but that's all. The casting director, on the other hand, is hired specifically to audition and cast the players.

Q. *Does the casting director book talent directly, or does she work through an agent or agents?*

A. Both. The casting director may call an agency and request to see actors of a certain type, and she may also put out a general call for an audition, at which both agented and non-agented talent are welcome.

Q. *What percentage of your fee does the casting director retain?*

A. Unlike an agent, who retains approximately 15 percent of your fee, a casting director is paid by the production company and takes nothing from your pay at all. Therefore, if you're booked directly by a casting director and your fee is one hundred dollars, then you receive the full one hundred dollars. If you're booked by a casting director through an agent, the agent receives the usual percentage.

An added benefit of being booked directly by a casting director is that you're paid directly by the client, so you receive your check much more quickly than when it is forwarded to you via an agent.

Q. *How do I find out if there are any casting directors in my area?*

A. Check the yellow pages. Casting directors will be listed under "modeling/talent agencies" or "casting directors." You can also try calling an agency and asking for names of the casting directors in your area.

Q. *Once I've found a casting director, how do I approach him?*

A. Similar to the way you would approach an agent: call the casting director; tell him you'd like to show him your photos; and relate an applicable experience you've had. He may ask you to send in a photo or to come in for an interview. Depending on what your special area of talent is, he may ask you to bring a prepared reading, to read cold, or to sing or dance for your interview. Then he will file your photo and resume and call you if any auditions come up for which he thinks you might be suitable.

Q. *How can I keep abreast of auditions?*

A. Once you're on the casting director's file, he'll call you if anything appropriate comes up. If he "puts out a call," your agent will let you know about it.

TWENTY-SEVEN

YOUR FIRST JOB

Your phone rings. You answer it. It's your agent calling to say that she's got a job for you! That audition you went to two weeks ago paid off; even though you didn't get the job you auditioned for, the art director remembered your face, and she wants you to be a customer in line at a bank teller window for a b&w print ad. Your agent tells you to bring two different outfits: shorts with a T-shirt and thongs, and a somewhat less casual combination of a blouse and slacks with sandals. Call time is 5:30 P.M. The shoot won't be at a studio, but rather on location at a bank after business hours. So, for security reasons, you'll have to stop at your agency on the way to the shoot to get a pass identifying you as a talent member. You thank your agent, hang up the phone . . . and panic! What should you do first?

LOCATE YOUR DESTINATION ON A MAP

Even if your agent provides you with directions to your booking, locate it on a map. If you don't have a map, buy one. If you don't know how to read one, it's time to learn.

I will never forget the time I was almost two hours late for an audition because I got the wrong directions from my agent. When I finally arrived at the client's office, I had wilted from the heat and frustration of driving around in rush hour traffic. Needless to say, I didn't get the job.

Unfortunate episodes like this one are not uncommon. They happen every day. And you know what? It's not the agent's fault. You are the professional. It's your responsibility to find the audition or booking and to arrive on time. The only way to do that is to know exactly where you're going in the first place. Hence, the map.

LEAVE YOURSELF PLENTY OF TIME

Your call time is 5:30. That means you have to be in the door of the bank no later than 5:15. You have to stop at the agency to pick up your security pass. It will be rush hour, and it may be hard to find parking. Estimate how long all this will take you, then add fifteen minutes to a half an hour onto that for good measure. Remember, it's no sin to arrive early, but you may never work for that client again if you arrive late. If you do arrive terribly early and the photographer isn't ready for you yet, stay out of the way and wait quietly. Or, if necessary, kill a few minutes at a nearby coffee shop or book store.

WARDROBE

As soon as you finish reading your map and planning your time frame, pack your wardrobe. Wear the shorts outfit, and carry the pants and blouse. While you're going through your closet, if you spot a sundress that you think fits the casual mode in which you've been asked to dress, pack that, too. If you think sunglasses and a folded newspaper would be a nice touch, bring them. The more the photographer has to choose from for your wardrobe, the happier he'll be.

MAKEUP

Leave yourself a little extra time to do your makeup and hair. After all, this is your first job, and you'll probably want to take a little more care. Also, you might be a bit clumsy if you're nervous. As your agent told you, this is a b&w shoot, so do your makeup accordingly.

WHEN YOU ARRIVE

You show up at the bank at 5:00 sharp. Now you have to let someone know you're there. Chances are you'll see a swarm of people all looking like they know where they're supposed to be, and you won't know who to talk to. Avoid bothering the director or photographer, who are probably setting up the shoot and attending to a million little details. Look, instead, for someone who is directing traffic flow and is possibly holding a clipboard. This is bound to be the art director or an assistant. She'll direct you to a spot where you can wait out of the way with the rest of the talent until someone comes to go over your wardrobe with you.

You'll probably find, to your surprise, that neither of the outfits you were asked to bring is chosen; instead, you wind up in the sundress and sunglasses you had the foresight to bring along. If there is a makeup artist present, she'll probably glance over you just to make sure your makeup is all right. Don't feel bad if she makes a little change or two.

Setting Up the Shot You'll be placed in your position for the shot and asked to stay there while the photographer meters the light and attends to last minute details. Some art directors allow quiet chatting on the set; others require silence. Try to sense the director's mood.

Shooting Pay complete attention to the art director or photographer and don't be afraid to give him what he requests. Some photographers welcome creative input from the models; and some want more control. It's up to you to anticipate his needs. *Cooperation* is the key word.

Wrapping Up When the art director says "That's a wrap" or "Thank you, that's all," look at your watch. Record the exact time on your voucher or the notebook you brought along for record keeping. You get paid from your call time (not your arrival time) to the second you hear the last click of the camera. So if the last shot was taken at 6:44, you record 6:44, not 6:45 or 6:50.

After the Wrap After the wrap, find the art director or assistant, and have her sign your voucher. You'll also sign a model's release at this time. If you have any questions about when and where the ad will run and whether you can get tear sheets, ask.

Reporting If your agency operates on the voucher system, have a stamped, addressed envelope with you at all times, and mail it on your way home from the shoot. If you phone your hours in, do it as soon as you get home. Don't put it off. Then congratulate yourself! You've had your first professional modeling job!

While no bookings will ever be typical or predictable, this scenario should help you anticipate at least some of what will happen.

TWENTY-EIGHT

REJECTION

No one likes being rejected, but it's a normal part of life. And in the field of modeling, even the best and most established people occasionally get rejected. You're bound to feel the sting of rejection sooner or later—probably sooner.

How do experienced models deal with rejection? What do agents really mean when they say, "I'll call you"? When should you take the criticism to heart and use it to make strategic changes? When should you ignore it? How much rejection should you submit yourself to before you simply throw in the towel? Here is a wealth of advice from models, agents, and others in the business.

HOW DO YOU KNOW WHEN THEY MEAN NO?

"We never tell anyone that they have no hope in this business or that we absolutely have no interest in them," said Mary, an agent. "You're dealing with a very emotional situation here, and no one likes to hurt people. So if we're really not interested in someone, we might tell them we already have enough models of their type or that they should try other agencies."

"Sometimes when I see someone I can't use due to a sensitive reason, such as bad skin or teeth or build, I'll tell her I can't use her, but I'll say it's because of something less sensitive like height or type," said a print booker named Julie.

"This business is just too expensive to string someone along who has no potential. I always level with people—as gently as possible, of course—so they aren't falsely encouraged to go out and spend more money on photos and promotional material," said Andrea, an agency owner.

So if you're not likely to get a simple, direct no from an agent, how will you know if they're truly not interested in you and that you should move on? What should you do if you've gotten a noncommittal or hard-to-interpret response and you're genuinely unsure whether you'll ever hear from this agent again or whether you would be welcome to call her?

"Ask me flat out. If you're direct, I'll be direct. Say, 'Do you think you can get me work?' If I don't think I can, I'll tell you," Julie said.

"It can't hurt to ask if you're not sure. I figure I should let people down as easily as possible, but if they have the courage to ask a direct question, I think they deserve a direct answer," said Mary.

Sometimes agents will list a person whom they're unsure about. They'll send out a few comps or photos to test the water. In this case, if their response seems ambiguous, it's because that's how they really feel. They're not just trying to let you down easy; they're really not sure whether they'll be able to have a working relationship with you or not. So don't always assume that "We'll give it a try and call you if anything comes up" is really a veiled no.

THE CONDITIONAL YES

Sometimes an agent will tell you, "Yes, I'll register you *if. . . .*" If you change your hairstyle, if you lose five pounds, if you have your teeth bonded, if you get new photos, or if you shave your beard. Should you take this criticism to heart and make a change or two with the hope of getting modeling work? Or should you ignore the suggestions?

The agents you talk to are just people, not all-seeing oracles. Their opinions are based on experience and know-how in their field, but they are still just opinions. Appearance, beauty, marketability—all are subjective judgments. Therefore, you should consider the suggestions carefully before making changes. Don't do anything that doesn't meet the following criteria:

1. You have heard the comment from more than one source. Treat it as sort of a democratic vote: if only one agent tells you to get a new hairstyle, put it on the back burner for now. But if two or more people in the business tell you that you need a new style, it could be a beneficial change.

2. You would feel comfortable with the change. For instance, if an agent tells you she'll represent you if you lose weight, but you think you would have a hard time maintaining that lower weight or that it would be unhealthy, then don't do it, even if all the agents in the city tell you the same thing. If you do, you'll only regret it. Even if you forfeit modeling work as a result of being unwilling to make that change, you'll be happier in the long run for being true to yourself.

3. When you're being honest with yourself, you can see the agent's point. Sometimes an agent will make a suggestion that might hurt you, but when you level with yourself, you have to admit that she's right. If this is the case, you might benefit from following her advice. Even if it doesn't get you any modeling work it might enhance your appearance and self-esteem.

Don't make a change based on just one person's opinion if it conflicts with your own or if it's a change that would make you unhappy.

"I've been told in the same week by various agents that I'm too thin, too big, too young, and too old. If I tried to please all of them I'd be a short fat bald thin man with lots of hair," said a character model. "So I just please myself."

"I've lost out on voice work because I'm black," said a model, "and then I turn around and lose a job because I don't sound black enough. There's just no predicting."

"I was advised by my agent to have my teeth worked on and to develop some more muscle tone. I did it, and I'm pleased as punch," said Lee.

"My agents both told me I'd get more work if I cut my hair shorter. So I did. And I didn't," said William.

What if you and your agent agree about your appearance, your portfolio and comp please both of you, and you get some auditions, but none of them results in a job. Some crazy things can run through your head if you let them.

"I've been in the business for nine years, and I still get a twinge when I lose an audition. I think, 'Is there anything I should have said or done differently? What were the magic words that could have gotten me that job?' "

"I think, 'Oh shoot, who's going to buy the groceries this week?' " said another model, John. "It's not so much my ego that's hurt as it is my pocketbook."

"I always relive the audition and do my best performance afterwards in the parking lot because, of course, the pressure's off, and what have I got to lose?"

"I think, 'Who got it?," said Eve. "What did she have that I don't? I should have worn my lucky sweater!' "

THINGS TO REMEMBER

No one ever gets used to rejection. But there are some things to remind yourself that can help you feel better when it happens:

● When you go to an audition, the client is trying to find a specific look. When you aren't chosen, it's not necessarily because you're less talented or less attractive than the person who was; it just means you weren't the type the client was looking for.

● When you go to a go-see, you're not presenting your whole self, and you're not baring your soul; you're simply trying to sell a product.

● This is not the only audition you'll ever have a crack at. You'll have many more chances.

● Don't blame yourself. Allow yourself to feel disappointment that you didn't get the job, and then forget it. No whipping yourself, and no self-pity. You'll do better next time, or the time after that.

In all the areas of our lives, rejection always hurts a little, no matter how tough we like to think we are. But it can be managed; rejection shouldn't be allowed to ruin your self-esteem—nor even your day.

TWENTY-NINE

WRAPPING IT UP

Now the secret is out: almost anyone can be a model. Regardless of age, type, sex, ethnicity, or occupation. And you can do it right in your own hometown; you don't have to move to New York City, L.A., or even Chicago. In fact, there are many benefits to staying right where you are, including a broader range of work for nonfashion types, less competition, smaller expenses, a more reasonable pace, and more accessible agents.

True, the work is usually only part-time, but can you think of many other part-time jobs that pay $20 to $125 an hour? And the other rewards—personal satisfaction, excitement, meeting new people, and breaking out of your daily grind—would all make modeling worthwhile, even if it paid less.

There is some financial investment involved, but this is true of most businesses. You can get your foot in the door at a reputable agency for very low cost if you 1) forgo modeling school and educate yourself through independent study, 2) practice shooting photos with friends to learn how different tones in makeup and wardrobe photograph, 3) study ads and practice in the mirror to learn posing and facial expression, 4) study your market to find your most salable looks and cultivate your own versions of these, and 5) learn to do your own hair and makeup. You can begin modeling for as little as the price of a few practice rolls of film, some cosmetics, a good haircut, and professional head shots.

The agent is your promoter, protector, adviser, and fee setter. Whenever possible, work through an agent rather than as a freelancer. But if you're forced to freelance, protect yourself by being as professional as you can. Don't sell yourself short; bill the client for what you think you're worth. Establish payment and a fee schedule in advance, and refuse to deal with clients who haven't paid their bills or who habitually pay late.

Whether you freelance or are represented by an agent, photographs are your most valuable promotional tool. You must take extreme care when choosing a photographer, designing your shoot, choosing the right looks, and considering the needs of your particular market.

You can keep your financial outlay to a minimum by starting out your modeling career with just two or three basic shots, and building your portfolio and composite as you gain experience and get modeling jobs.

Print models sometimes cross over into broadcast modeling. Broadcast modeling requires more training and expertise, but the pay is excellent and the work can be enjoyable and challenging.

So why wait any longer? With a minimal investment, you could be in business for yourself as a model in print ads for fashion and nonfashion products and services, in industrial films and slide shows, in TV commercials biting into hamburgers, live in gorgeous fashions on the runway, or on billboards or posters. There's never been a better time to go for it!

GLOSSARY

Actor: A general term referring to film, stage, and broadcast performers.

AFTRA: The American Federation of Television and Radio Artists; the union which you are most likely to be asked to join if you become a broadcast model.

Agent: One who represents and promotes models and actors.

Audition: A trial performance for broadcast actors, or a simple interview and showing of the portfolio for print models.

Bleed-Off: The area immediately outside of the camera frame, which is cut off and cannot be seen in the final photo or video.

Body shot: A full-length photograph of a model to show the build and physical condition of the model's body. A woman usually wears a bathing suit, leotard, or lingerie for her body shot. A man wears no shirt, or wears a revealing tank or T-shirt with jeans, shorts, or bathing trunks.

Book: A model's portfolio.

Booker: A modeling agent or talent agent.

Booking: A modeling or broadcast job. "I have a booking for Tuesday at 11:00 A.M. for XYZ store."

Broadcast model: An actor who performs in commercials, industrial films and other audiovisual presentations.

Cattle call: A large audition at which the client may see literally hundreds of models and/or actors.

Character model: Like a character ac-tor, a character model portrays stereotyped or unusual people for print.

Comp or composite photo: A single sheet with two to five photos printed on one or both sides. It includes the model's name and vital statistics. It is used as a promotional tool and shows the model's range of looks.

Contact sheet: One sheet of photo paper with negative-sized prints from an entire roll of film. It is also called a "proof sheet." Models use it to choose which shots from a photo session to blow up into 8x10s.

Cropping: Changing the composition of a photo negative in the printing process to achieve a more dramatic or desirable effect.

Day rate: The rate of pay a model makes for working five or more hours in one day.

Dress shield: Small, thin pads which are worn inside a dress or blouse in the underarm area, to prevent staining the clothing with perspiration.

Exclusive listing: When you have a contractual agreement to be represented by only one agency, you have an exclusive listing.

Fashion model: One who models clothing, jewelry and accessories for ads, editorial spreads and live shows.

Fashion shot: A photograph of a model wearing fashion clothing intended to demonstrate her ability to pose and to project a mood or attitude that shows the clothing well.

Fee schedule: A determination of the basis on which you will be paid (i.e., a flat fee, an hourly wage, or a day rate), when you will be paid, and by whom, for modeling or broadcast work.

Go-see: See *audition*.

Head shot: A photograph of the model's head and shoulders.

Headsheet or headbook: A promotional tool used by modeling/talent agencies to promote their models to clients. Usually a poster or bound book of photos of talent divided into different categories, i.e., children, men, women and fashion.

Industrial print model: A model who is a spokesperson or average type, not a fashion model and not a character model. This type of model usually appears as a young parent, businessperson or other professional person, or a homeowner.

Introductory head shot: A model's first and most important promotional tool. A head shot shows the model smiling into the camera, head-on with minimal accessories, simple hairstyle and clothing, and soft lighting.

List: To enter into a verbal or written contractual agreement in which the agent agrees to represent and promote you as a model or actor, in return for a percentage of your earnings.

Model: A general term referring to those who appear in fashion, industrial, and character roles in print or broadcast.

Modeling agent: A term used interchangeably with *talent agent*. It is usually an agent who represents fashion and other types of print models.

MOR: Stands for "middle of the road," meaning an average, pleasant appearance which is desirable for industrial models.

Multiple Listing: When you are registered with more than one modeling/talent agency, you have a multiple listing.

Overexposure: When a model has appeared too frequently in one market, he can become overexposed, and therefore undesirable to potential clients.

Portfolio: A collection of a professional model's photographs and samples of her work.

Principal: A featured player in a television commercial or industrial film or video.

Proof sheet: See *contact sheet*.

Register: See *list*.

Residuals: Money paid to an actor for each 13 week period that a commercial in which he appears runs in a given market. This is payment he receives above and be-

yond his initial fee for appearing in the commercial.

SAG: Screen Actor's Guild, a sister union to AFTRA.

Scale: The minimum rate of pay as determined by AFTRA and SAG.

Set-up: In a photo session, each different series of photos involving a change of set, location, props, or composition is a set-up.

Shoot: A photo session.

Spots: A spot refers to an ad or a part of an ad; i.e., "Have you seen the new spot on TV showing the fire alarm system?", or, "I just taped a voice-over spot for Yum-Yum doggie treats."

Stats: Statistics that appear on a model's composite photo, usually including hair and eye color, height, weight, clothing sizes and special talents.

Talent: A term mainly referring to broadcast actors, but also referring to print models.

Talent agent: A term often used interchangeably with *modeling agent*. It is most

often an agent who represents and promotes broadcast actors.

Tear sheet: Samples of a model's work: photographs clipped from actual newspapers, magazines, and other published material.

Test shoot: A trial photo session in which the photographer, model, and designers agree to waive their fees and work together for free or for a portion of the expense of the film and processing.

Tone: Degree of light or darkness of make-up, clothing, skin, background, and objects as they appear when photographed on black and white film.

Trunk shows: Informal, live fashion shows often held in small boutiques or in clothing sections of department stores.

Vital statistics: Information about a model that is usually included on her resume and composite photo: name, height, weight, clothing sizes or measurements, and special talents. Vital statistics are often called stats.

Wrap: A term used to indicate the end of a photo session, i.e., "That's a wrap!"

INDEX

Other Books to Help You Make Money
and the Most of Your Talents